Suicide in Children and Adolescents

MOTHER

Through the eyes of childhood
the visions of my adulthood,
my perceptions were shaped by you.
So casually you dropped words
to weight upon me;
they became the roots of my imagination.
I clung to their meaning,
watching from behind you
as you did your daily work,
in your exact and patient way.
How I wished
that you would turn from your tasks
just to hug me.
Perhaps you wished that you could;
perhaps you have wished that you had?

FATHER

Does the child's reality
greet the man;
or does it sit in his soul
waiting to fly
and free his spirit
from the daily drudge,
long enough to permit time
to fly a kite
while his children shout
and laugh and experience love.

Norma Young

Suicide
in Children and Adolescents

Edited by
George MacLean, M.D.

Ottawa, Ontario, Canada

Hogrefe & Huber Publishers

Toronto • Lewiston, NY • Bern • Göttingen • Stuttgart

Library of Congress Cataloging-in-Publication Data

Suicide in children and adolescents / George MacLean, editor.
    p.   cm.
  Includes bibliographical references.
  ISBN 0-920887-52-X
  1. Children — Suicidal behavior. 2. Teenagers — Suicidal behavior. 3. Child
psychotherapy. 4. Adolescent psychotherapy. I. MacLean, George, 1939-
RJ506.S9S85 1990
618.92'858445 — dc20
90-19880
CIP

Canadian Cataloguing in Publication Data

Main entry under title:
Suicide in children and adolescents

Includes bibliographical references.
ISBN 0-920887-52-X

1. Children — Suicidal behavior. 2. Youth — Suicidal behavior. 3. Depression in
children. I. MacLean, George, 1939-

RJ506.S9S94 1990   618.92'858445   C90-094965-4

Printed in the United States of America

ISBN 0-920887-52-X
Hogrefe & Huber Publishers • Toronto • Lewiston NY • Göttingen • Bern • Stuttgart
ISBN 3-456-81823-8
Hans Huber Publishers • Bern • Stuttgart • Toronto • Lewiston N.Y

To Norma, Calvin, Ryan and Jennifer

About the Contributors

Simon Davidson, M.D.
Assistant Professor, Division of Child and Adolescent Psychiatry, School of Medicine, University of Ottawa; Director of Child Psychiatric Research, Childrens Hospital of Eastern Ontario, Ottawa, Ontario.

Russell T. Joffe, M.D.
Assistant Professor, Department of Psychiatry, University of Toronto; Director, Mood Disorders Clinic and Research Program, St. Michael's Hospital, Toronto, Ontario.

George MacLean, M.D.
Clinical Associate Professor, Division of Child and Adolescent Psychiatry, Department of Psychiatry, School of Medicine, University of Ottawa; Staff Psychiatrist, Ottawa General Hospital; Consultant Psychiatrist, Childrens Hospital of Eastern Ontario, Ottawa, Ontario.

David R. Offord, M.D.
Professor of Psychiatry and Head, Division of Child Psychiatry, Department of Psychiatry, McMaster University, Research Director, Child and Family Centre, Chedoke-McMaster Hospitals, Hamilton, Ontario.

Cynthia R. Pfeffer, M.D.
Associate Professor of Clinical Psychiatry, Cornell University Medical College; Chief, Child Psychiatry Inpatient Unit, New York Hospital—Westchester Division, White Plains, New York.

TABLE OF CONTENTS

Editor's Foreword

When I started my residency in child psychiatry in a large training program in a metropolitan center, I began to meet with many children and even more adolescents who had attempted to commit suicide. In the necessary flow through the busy emergency department, usually such patients would be tersely evaluated by a pediatric resident and then sent to the child psychiatry unit. Successful suicides, like so many other clinical realities, I confronted only after graduation. Children do kill themselves!

One seven-year-old patient of mine tried to hang himself, and was almost successful. I had been treating the boy and his family, with the therapy centering on aiding a single parent, as usual the mother. She was attempting to deal with a severely hearing-impaired three-year-old boy and two older children, this child and a girl of nine. The younger boy was receiving everyone's attention, while the girl seemed to have no problem captivating anyone. We had not realized that the seven-year-old thought that death offered a reasonable solution.

I continued my treatment of the family, and I rushed to the library, pointed in that direction by my lack of knowledge on the topic. My review of the literature at that time showed that there had been a long historical interest in suicide in children and adolescents, and that this interest was obviously increasing.

In the fifteen years since my residency, knowledge of depression among children and adolescents has increased. As with many problems of morbidity and mortality, we are quickly becoming more aware that depression exists among the young, that it is common, and that it is a major, specific risk factor for suicide.

What is known about the subject of youth suicide will be condensed here for the nonspecialist clinician. All professionals who work with children should know of the seriousness of the problem, the basic facts of its epidemiology, and its clinical presentation. They should be clear on the assessment of the manifestations of risk of suicide in this age group, in particular the role of depression. They should know how to treat the suicidal child in the context of his or her family. Finally, they should be aware of means of prevention. They must know all this because, despite the reality of under-reporting and the continued confusion over definitions of suicide and of children's concepts of death, children are dying. It is a tragedy that we continue to read of more fully reported suicides among young people in the newspapers than we do in clinical reports.

Whatever their age or their level of cognitive development, all children have some sort of concept of death, and it is a fact that they may attempt to kill themselves or succeed in doing so with their particular concept in operation. In the United States, suicide is the third most common cause of death for 15- to 24-year-olds after accidents and homicides, and both these other forms of violent death are suspect in some cases as disguised suicides or as having suicidal motivation. Suicide is not even classified as a possible cause of death for children under the age of 10 by the U.S. Center for Health Statistics, but we know that it is the tenth leading cause in the 5- to 14-year-old age group.

The first chapter of this book details the epidemiology of suicidal behavior in children and adolescents in a statistical review that is shocking but instructive. Chapter 2 presents some clinical realities of the problem. Chapter 3 discusses depression in some detail because of its important link with suicide in this age group. The fourth chapter outlines in a simple and practical manner the manifestations of suicidal risk, while the final chapter describes the spectrum and integration of treatments.

It is hoped that this approach will provide clinicians with the essential facts necessary for their work with children and families. We must know the facts of epidemiology, facts of clinical importance, facts of depression, facts of assessment of risk, and facts of treatment and prevention — for too many children are dying!

George MacLean, M.D., FRCPC
Ottawa, Canada
September, 1989

Chapter 1

Epidemiology

Russell T. Joffe, M.D., and David R. Offord, M.D.

Suicide and suicide attempts in children and adolescents have been increasingly identified as important clinical and public health problems. In the United States there has been a marked increase over the last 25 years in the rate of completed suicide, and it is now the third leading cause of death during the adolescent age span (Holinger, 1978; 1979). There has been a dramatic increase in Canada as well (Health and Welfare Canada, 1987). Along with the death statistics, there is the disturbing fact that suicidal behavior—ideation and attempts—in youth is far more common than the completed act (Joffe & Offord, 1983).

This chapter reviews the prevalence rates for both suicidal behavior and completed suicide in childhood and adolescence. The demographic aspects will be evaluated, with a distinction drawn between children (defined as 12 years and younger) and adolescents (13 or older). The two main types of studies on the psychosocial and clinical correlates of suicidal acts are reviewed: the first (comprising the majority) involving inpatient or outpatient clinical populations, and the second involving children from community samples who have not presented for psychiatric treatment. Particular attention will be paid here to data obtained from the Ontario Child Health Study, a community interview survey carried out to evaluate the prevalence of psychiatric disorders amongst children in the province of Ontario, Canada.

Prevalence of Attempted and Completed Suicide

Between 1960 and 1985 there was a substantial (two to threefold) increase in the rate of completed suicides in Canada for both males and females in the age groups 10 to 14 years and 15 to 19 years (Health and Welfare Canada, 1987). The rate of completed suicides increased similarly in the United States. No statistics are kept for completed suicide in children under the age of ten in either of these countries, but the act has been well documented in latency age children (Shaffer & Fisher, 1981). All statistics on completed suicides are probably underestimates, with some deaths reported as being due to accidents or other causes. This may be particularly so with young victims, because of the social stigma involved and the need to protect the family.

In Canada, between 1960 and 1985 there was an approximate twofold increase in the rate of completed suicides among males aged 10 to 14 and among both males and females in the 15- to 19-year-old age group; and a six-fold increase in females aged 10 to 14. In both age groups, completed suicide was substantially more common in males (Holinger & Luke, 1984). These statistics are very comparable to those in the United States (Holinger, 1978, 1979; Holinger & Luke, 1984).

All the North American statistics do not even take into account the incidence of other types of suicidal behavior such as ideation, threats, and attempts, which are much more common than completed suicide. The ratio of attempted to completed suicide has been estimated at from 50:1 (Jacobziner, 1960) to 120:1 (Tuckman & Connon, 1962). Most of the prevalence estimates are derived from studies carried out on clinical populations, particularly from psychiatric outpatient departments.

Several reports from the late 1960s (Lukianowicz, 1968; Mattson, Seese, & Hawkins, 1969; Shaffer, 1974) reported that up to 10% of children referred to pediatric outpatient psychiatric clinics presented with suicidal behavior. In contrast, in a more recent study Pfeffer and collaborators (1980) found evidence of this in 33% of children presenting at the Bronx Municipal Hospital clinic. This difference in prevalence rates between the earlier and later studies may be interpreted in one of two ways: it may represent a true increase in the frequency of suicidal attempts in child psychiatric populations over the years (which would be consistent with the increased prevalence of completed suicides over this same period of time), or it may be due to methodological issues such as sample selection and the definition and ascertainment of suicidal behavior.

There are very limited data on the prevalence of suicidal behaviors in nonpsychiatric childhood populations. Pfeffer and colleagues (1984), in a study of 101 randomly selected schoolchildren with no history of psychiatric illness, found that 11.9% of them reported suicidal behavior and 1% had made an actual attempt. Conclusions from this study are limited by the fact that the community sample was generated by finding matched control subjects for an inpatient psychiatric sample, and therefore was not representative of the general population. Friedman and colleagues (1987), with a sample of 380 high school students attending an academically select public high school in New York, found that 60% reported that they thought of killing themselves and 8.7% had made an attempt. These data are impressive as they indicate a very high prevalence of suicidal behavior in a non-clinical population; however, their generalizability is limited by the selective nature of the academically competitive type of school from which they were obtained. In addition, as with most community studies the data were derived by means of a checklist, and the meaning of such findings and the extent to which they are comparable to that elicited by a clinical interview are problematic issues.

The prevalence of suicidal behavior in community populations was also looked at in the Ontario Child Health Study, a cross-sectional interview survey of 1,869 families including 3,294 children. Its primary objective was to provide precise and unbiased estimates of the prevalence of four psychiatric disorders (attention deficit disorder, emotional disorder, conduct disorder, and somatization disorder) amongst children aged 4 to 16 (Boyle et al., 1987; Offord et al., 1987). Data on suicidal behavior obtained from youths aged 12 to 16 found the prevalence to be 5% to 10% in the males and 10% to 20% in the females (Joffe, Offord, & Boyle, 1988). These findings are more generalizable to the population at large, not only to those receiving clinical services.

Demography

Age and Sex

Most studies agree that youth suicidal behavior increases with age, and that both attempts and completed suicide are more common in latency age males than females (Lukianowicz, 1968; Mattson, Seese, & Hawkins, 1969; Shaffer, 1974). In adolescence, the rate of suicidal attempts is significantly higher in females (Jacobziner, 1960; Mattson et al., 1969), with a dramatic increase in wrist-slashing and poison ingestion by girls aged 14 to 16 years (Bergstrand & Otto, 1962). Completed suicide remains more common in adolescent males (Holinger & Luke, 1984).

Socioeconomic Status

Several studies report increased rates of suicidal behavior in youngsters of lower socioeconomic status (Bergstrand & Otto, 1962; Lukianowicz, 1968). However, this may be an artifact of the clinical samples studied, as most were drawn from tertiary hospital clinics located in economically disadvantaged areas. They may also result from reporting differences: that is, suicide attempts may be recorded as such in lower socioeconomic groups but are claimed to be accidents in children of a higher social class. In the Ontario Child Health Study, economic disadvantage was not found to be an important independent predictor (Joffe, Offord, & Boyle, 1988).

Race and Religion

There are very limited data on the relationship between suicidal behavior in youth and race or religion, which may be due to the fact that most studies to date have involved small and biased clinical samples. Although some investigators (McIntyre & Angle, 1973) suggest that religious factors parallel those in adults, with suicidal behavior less common in Catholic than Protestant children, others report no differences (Gould, 1965; McIntyre & Angle, 1971, 1973). It has been suggested that suicidal behavior may be more common amongst Caucasian children (Balser & Masterson, 1959; McIntyre & Angle, 1973), but these study groups were derived from predominantly white populations. In two studies from poison control centers (reviewed in Joffe & Offord, 1983), the number of blacks was high; in a study of completed suicide in youth aged 10 to 14 years the rate in whites was considerably higher than in blacks (Shaffer, 1974). In summary, there are limited and contradictory data on this relationship.

Psychosocial Correlates

Psychiatric Diagnosis

There is little correlation in the literature between the spectrum of youth suicidal behavior and clinical psychiatric diagnosis, as studies are limited by the changing trends in the diagnosis of pediatric psychiatric disorders. Moreover, the correlates are dependent on the clinical sample studied; for example, there was a high incidence of schizophrenia in studies where samples were drawn from adolescent inpatients at state psychiatric hospitals (Balser & Masterson, 1959).

With regard to clinical populations, the most common diagnoses associated with suicide are behavioral disorders and neuroses of varying kinds (Lawler, Nakielny, & Wright, 1963; Lukianowicz, 1968; Mattson, Seese, & Hawkins, 1969; McIntyre & Angle, 1971). However, all these studies have been limited by inadequate control groups or nonstandardized diagnostic criteria, and more research is needed.

Most studies agree that depression — either the symptom, the psycho-dynamic phenomenon, or the clinical syndrome — is an important feature of suicidal behavior in childhood (Garfinkel & Golombek, 1974; Mattson, Seese, & Hawkins, 1969; Shaw & Schelkun, 1965; Toolan, 1975). In this regard, Mattson et al. found that 40% of 75 suicidal children versus 12% of 85 nonsuicidal children who presented as child psychiatric emergencies over a two-year period had shown features of depression one month before being evaluated. Pfeffer and colleagues (1979) reported that latency age children with suicidal behavior could be distinguished from age-matched controls by feelings of worthlessness, hopelessness, depression, and a wish to die. In adolescent clinical populations, the major features associated with suicide and parasuicide appear to be depression, borderline personality disorder, and substance abuse (Crumley, 1979).

Clinical correlates of suicidal behavior have also been examined in community studies. Pfeffer and colleagues (1984) found a greater preoccupation with death and more recent and past depression in nonclinical preadolescent schoolchildren who reported suicidal behavior. The results of the Ontario Child Health Study (Boyle et al., 1987; Joffe, Offord, & Boyle, 1988; Offord et al., 1987) were limited to more general findings about psychopathology because of the limiting methodology that made use of checklists. It was found that suicidal ideation and attempts in youths aged 12 to 16 were related to psychiatric disorder in general, rather than being specifically related to any of the four particular psychiatric disorders surveyed. The seriousness of suicidal behavior cannot be clearly evaluated using checklists. Therefore, it is impossible to relate seriousness to any specific psychiatric disorder. The finding that relates suicidal ideation and attempts to psychiatric disorder in general is the most that can be concluded and defended.

Family Variables

Family factors appear to be of importance in increasing the vulnerability to suicidal behavior in youngsters, with a high prevalence of broken homes by death, divorce, or separation reported in nearly every study from clinical samples (Lawler, Nakielny, & Wright, 1963; Lukianowicz, 1968; McIntyre & Angle, 1973; Shaffer, 1974). All these studies lacked control groups, however. Later studies (McIntyre & Angle, 1973; Pfeffer et al., 1979; Pfeffer et al., 1980) found no significant difference in the evidence of marital discord or parental loss in the families of suicidal as compared to nonsuicidal psychiatrically ill children.

Some clinical studies have reported a high incidence of mental illness, particularly suicidal behavior, in the parents of suicidal children (Bergstrand & Otto, 1962; Pfeffer et al., 1979; Shaffer, 1974). However, these studies were poorly controlled, and it remains to be determined whether maternal or paternal psychiatric illness is a risk factor for suicidal behavior specifically, or just for psychiatric illness in general. Many of the family factors that have been described as risk factors for suicidal behavior in children are similar to the six major risk factors of childhood psychopathology defined by Trotter (1981): low socioeconomic class, material psychiatric illness, paternal delinquency, large families and overcrowding, marital discord and broken homes, and institutional care.

In the Ontario Child Health Study, the independent contribution of parental arrest and family dysfunction as predictors of suicidal behavior in adolescents was noted. It was concluded that family dysfunction and current psychiatric disorder were more important factors than the amount of economic resources available, while parental mental illness was not found to make a significant independent contribution.

Thus, with regard to family factors the clinical studies (which were poorly controlled) suggest that specific aspects of family dysfunction are of importance, but these findings are not supported by community studies. Further studies on well defined clinical samples using proper control groups are required to identify whether there are specific family factors that increase the risk of suicidal behavior in children and adolescents, independent of those for childhood psychiatric disorders in general.

Interpersonal Functioning

A few studies have tended to describe suicidal youths as being isolated with poor social skills (Garfinkel & Golombek, 1974). However, these studies are limited by the lack of control groups, and suggest that, as with other psychosocial correlates, poor interpersonal skills may be more a risk factor for psychiatric disorders in general rather than specifically for suicidal behavior.

Most studies report that, despite normal intellect, suicidal children and adolescents function poorly at school (Connell, 1972; Rosenberg & Latimer, 1966). However, in two controlled studies, poor school performance and learning disabilities did not distinguish suicidal from nonsuicidal age-matched psychiatric controls (Pfeffer et al., 1979), although they did distinguish single suicide attempters from repeaters (Stanley & Barter, 1970). School performance and interpersonal relationships are fundamental aspects of the function of children and adolescents, and further research to evaluate their relationship to suicidal behavior should yield important clinical and therapeutic information.

Methods of Suicide

It is generally agreed that in both inpatient and outpatient psychiatric populations, violent methods in suicidal attempts are used more often by latency age children than by either adolescents or even adults. These methods include hanging, stabbing, burning, jumping from heights, and running into traffic; firearms however are seldom if ever used (Lukianowicz, 1968; Pfeffer et al., 1980). In contrast to attempts, completed suicide in children is usually by different methods, particularly gassing, ingestion, and firearms (Shaffer, 1974). This difference in methods may be helpful in distinguishing the seriousness of intentionality of these two groups.

Among adolescents ingestion is very common (Bergstrand & Otto, 1962), largely attributable to females aged 14 to 16 who frequently attempt suicide by drug overdose.

Conclusions

Suicidal behavior, including both attempted and completed acts, is becoming an increasing problem in both children and adolescents. Data on the clinical and psychosocial correlates are drawn largely from psychiatrically ill populations, where conclusions are limited by methodological flaws such as inadequate sample collections, lack of precise definition of current diagnostic criteria, and lack of control groups. The data on community samples are limited by the fact that these studies are cross-sectional in nature and therefore do not allow a closer evaluation of the temporal sequence between suicidal behavior and its correlates. Further studies in both populations with attention paid to methodological inadequacies and follow-up are required. In particular, in community studies, the meaningfulness of checklist data collection and its clinical significance requires further examination.

Recommended Reading

Holinger, P.C., & Luke, K.W. (1984). The epidemiologic patterns of self-destructiveness in childhood, adolescence and young adulthood. In H.S. Sudak, A.B. Ford, & N.B. Rushfort (Eds.), *Suicide in the young* (pp. 97-114). Boston: John Wright.

A good review of the spectrum of epidemiological concerns in this area.

Joffe, R.T., Offord, D.R., & Boyle, M.H. (1988). Ontario Child Health Study: Suicidal behavior in youth age 12-16 years. *American Journal of Psychiatry, 145,* 1420-1423.

Taken from a large epidemiological study, this work introduces students to the greater community concerns with suicide in this age group.

Pfeffer, C.R., Conte, H.R., Plutchik, R., & Jerrert, I. (1980). Suicidal behavior in latency age children: An outpatient population. *Journal of the American Academy of Child Psychiatry, 19,* 703-710.

A careful look at the spectrum of suicidal behavior in a more specific population of risk.

Shaffer, D. (1974). Suicide in childhood and early adolescence. *Journal of Child Psychology and Psychiatry, 15,* 275-391.

A classic study that should be read as a basic prerequisite to all others.

Shaffer, D., & Fisher, P. (1981). The epidemiology of suicide in children and adolescence. *Journal of the American Academy of Child Psychiatry, 21,* 545-566.

A thorough review.

References

Balser, B.H., & Masterson, J.F. (1959). Suicide in adolescence. *American Journal of Psychiatry, 115,* 400-404.

Bergstrand, C.G., & Otto, U. (1962). Suicide attempts in adolescence and childhood. *Acta Pediatrica, 51,* 17-26.

Boyle, M.H., Offord, D.R., Hofmann, H.G., Catlin, G.P., Byles, J.A., Cadman, D.T., Crawford, J.W., Links, P.S., Rae-Grant, N.I., & Szatmari, P. (1987). Ontario Child Health Study, I: Methodology. *Archives of General Psychiatry, 44,* 826-831.

Connell, H.M. (1972). Attempted suicide in school children. *Medical Journal of Australia, 1,* 686-690.

Crumley, F.E. (1979). Adolescent suicide attempts. *Journal of the American Medical Association, 241,* 2404-2407.

Friedman, J.M.H, Asnis, G.M., Boeck, M., & Difiore, J. (1987). Prevalence of specific suicidal behaviors in a high school sample. *American Journal of Psychiatry, 144,* 1203-1206.

Garfinkel, B.D., & Golombek, H. (1974). Suicide and depression in childhood and adolescence. *Canadian Medical Association Journal, 110,* 1278-1281.

Gould, R.E. (1965). Suicide problems in children and adolescents. *American Journal of Psychotherapy, 19,* 228-246.

Health and Welfare Canada (1987). *Suicide in Canada.* Reports of the National Task Force on Suicide in Canada.

Holinger, P.C. (1978). Adolescent suicide: An epidemiologic study of recent trends. *Amer. J. Psychiatry, 135,* 754-756.

Holinger, P.C. (1979). Violent death among the young: Recent trends in suicide, homicide and accidents. *American Journal of Psychiatry, 136,* 1144-1147.

Holinger, P.C., & Luke, K.W. (1984). The epidemiologic patterns of self-destructiveness in childhood, adolescence and young adulthood. In H.S. Sudak, A.B. Ford, & N.B. Rushfort (Eds.), *Suicide in the young* (pp. 97-114). Boston: John Wright.

Jacobziner, H. (1960). Attempted suicide in children. *Journal of Pediatrics, 56,* 519-525.

Joffe, R.T., & Offord, D.R. (1983). Suicidal behavior in childhood. *Canadian Journal of Psychiatry, 28,* 57-63.

Joffe, R.T., Offord, D.R, & Boyle, M.H. (1988). Ontario Child Health Study: Suicidal behavior in youth age 12-16 years. *American Journal of Psychiatry, 145,* 1420-1423.

Lawler, R.H., Nakielny,W., & Wright, N.A. (1963). Suicidal attempts in children. *Canadian Medical Association Journal, 89,* 751-754.

Lukianowicz, N. (1968) Attempted suicide in children. *Acta Psychiatrica Scandinavia, 44,* 415-435.

Mattson, A., Seese, R.S., & Hawkins J.W. (1969). Suicidal behavior as a child psychiatric emergency. *Archives of General Psychiatry, 20,* 100-109.

McIntyre, M.S., & Angle, C.R. (1971). Suicide as seen in a poison control centre. *Pediatrics, 48,* 914-922.

McIntyre, M.S., & Angle, C.R. (1973). Psychological "biopsy" in self-poisoning of children and adolescents. *American Journal of Diseases of Children, 126,* 42-46.

Offord, D.R., Boyle, M.H., Szatmari, P., Rae-Grant, N.I., Links, P.S., Cadman, D.T., Byles, J.A., Crawford, J.W., Blum, H.M., Byrne, C., Thomas, H., & Woodward, C.A. (1987). Ontario Child Health Study, II: Six month prevalence of disorder and rates of service utilization. *Archives of General Psychiatry, 44,* 831-835.

Pfeffer, C.R., Conte, H.R., Plutchik, R., & Jerrert, I. (1979). Suicidal behavior in latency age children. *Journal of the American Academy of Child Psychiatry, 18,* 679-692.

Pfeffer, C.R., Conte, H.R., Plutchik, R., & Jerrert, I. (1980). Suicidal behavior in latency age children: An outpatient population. *Journal of the American Academy of Child Psychiatry, 19,* 703-710.

Pfeffer, C.R., Zuckerman, S., Plutchik, R., & Mizruchi, M.S. (1984). Suicidal behavior in normal school children: A comparison with child psychiatric inpatients. *Journal of the American Academy of Child Psychiatry, 23,* 416-423.

Rosenberg, P.H., & Latimer, R. (1966). Suicide attempts by children. *Mental Hygiene, 50,* 354-359.

Shaffer, D. (1974) Suicide in childhood and early adolescence. *Journal of Child Psychology and Psychiatry, 15,* 275-391.

Shaffer, D, & Fisher, P. (1981). The epidemiology of suicide in children and adolescence. *Journal of the American Academy of Child Psychiatry, 21,* 545-566.

Shaw, C.R., & Schelkun, R.F. (1965). Suicidal behavior in children. *Psychiatry, 28,* 157-168.

Stanley, E.J., & Barter, J.T. (1970). Adolescent suicidal behavior. *American Journal of Orthopsychiatry, 40,* 87-95.

Toolan, J.M. (1975). Suicide in children and adolescence. *American Journal of Psychotherapy, 29,* 339-344.

Trotter, R.J. (1981). Psychiatry for the 80's. *Science News, 119,* 348-349.

Tuckman, J., & Connon, H.E. (1962). Attempted suicide in adolescence. *American Journal of Psychiatry, 119,* 228-232.

Chapter 2

Clinical Perspectives

George MacLean, M.D.

There is ample indication that the current interest in suicide and attempted suicide in children and adolescents is growing. In one early review of the literature (Lukianowicz, 1968), it was noted that articles describing cases of child suicide had been appearing for over 100 years. The first cases were described in French and German journals, which commented on the tendency of the problem to increase with the age of the victims and with urbanization and industrialization. Interest in the subject amongst English-speaking writers was of a much later onset, and was at first confined to American authors. In contrast, scanning the recent literature one finds a markedly pronounced interest, with hundreds of articles appearing every year in prominent journals.

What accounts for this interest? Clinicians dealing with children find that suicidal threats and attempts are commonly encountered in their practice: reports from various clinics are consistent in noting that ten percent of all referrals and an even larger proportion of cases seen as psychiatric emergencies have threatened or attempted suicide (Shaffer, 1974).

One problem noted in the literature is achieving greater clarification. Reports of suicide in children as distinct from adolescents are rare and for the most part the two groups have been considered together (Kofkin, 1979). It is only reasonable that children should be investigated and studied separately in order to clarify differences in causation, clinical manifestations, aspects of risk and different treatment approaches.

As described in Chaper 4 on risk factors, we emphasize that suidicidal behavior and suicide are complexities that do not involve a neat, discrete clinical entity, but rather represent symptomatic acts that have multiple causes in varying combinations (Gould, 1965).

A variety of opinions have been presented concerning the true incidence of attempted and successful suicide in children, as reviewed in Chapter 1 on epidemiology. There is the ever-present concern that the reported incidence is not reliable, so that although official statistics on completed suicide in children indicates that it is quite rare, the actual number is much higher (Gould, 1965). Particularly with young victims, there is a great reluctance to label death as self-induced unless there is no choice in the matter (Lourie, 1966). In many cases of threatened or attempted suicide in children, parents may not take the gesture seriously enough to seek professional advice. Some parents of victims, no matter how disturbed or upset, do not report the truth — afraid of publicity, social embarrassment, or disgrace, they hush up the incident. They may also fear an investigation and possible prosecution for neglect or cruelty (Kofkin, 1979).

Other factors noted to conspire to lower the recorded number of child suicides are the following (these factors vary inversely with age):

- The methods of suicide utilized by children often res_.. ... deaths classified as accidents, that is, self-poisoning, jumping from heights, or running into traffic.

- Children do not leave suicide notes.

- There is a tradition in our culture to underestimate the strengths of children's emotions, and suicidal motives of children are regarded as unthinkable (Lourie, 1966).

Children's accidents may very well correspond in this respect to automobile and firearm "accidents" of adolescents and adults (Kofkin, 1979). This is important to note since accidents are by a wide margin the leading cause of death in childhood and adolescence, and there is no way of knowing how many are disguised suicides. The results of one survey defended the opinion that self-poisoning of a child over the age of 6 is rarely accidental (McIntyre & Angle, 1970). That survey noted an increase in the United States of 34,000 to 116,000 cases of self-poisoning a year between the ages of 6 and 18.

Concepts of Death —
A Developmental Perspective

Anyone who has lived with children and has had any interest in observing their behavior and speech knows that from a very early age they have a particular interest in death. Whether it is the first dead bird found outside or the loss of the family pet, the questions asked by the young child are often very meaningful. As described by many authors, the initial concerns are very concrete and egocentric.

Any assessment of suicidal motivation in children must take into account the child's concept of death. However, when we try to find out what death may mean to children at varying stages of development, we find that formal inquiry into this has been relatively infrequent and there are few systematic data.

Dr. Hermine Hug-Hellmuth, the first child psychoanalyst, published the first paper on the topic in 1912, in German, entitled "The Child's Concept of Death." Although this was a very important paper, it did not appear in English until 1965, when Anton Kris published a translation of it in the *Psychoanalytic Quarterly*. MacLean and Rappen (in preparation) report that Hug-Hellmuth's own early development was disturbed by the death of two siblings, the death of her paternal grandmother, and, finally, the death of her mother when she was only thirteen years old. With our knowledge of her intimate acquaintance at an early age with several deaths in her immediate family, we can understand her pioneering work on this topic and her writing: "No event among the abundant phenomena of human life is insignificant for the child, in particular the beginning and the end of life, the entrance and exit of individuals are an inexhaustible source of his 'whys' and 'wherefores' ... [to the child, death may mean] a state of sleep from which one can be readily awakened." She discussed the fact that guilt is often associated with the death of a loved one, and noted the developmental process that culminates in children becoming aware of the fact that they are "not excluded from the universal rule of life and death." From the "egocentric infantile attitude" of children she related the development of "altruistic feelings," and described the psychodynamic aspects of infantile death wishes. She made extensive use of the work of nonpsychoanalytic observers of children, and from this she identified and clearly discussed death wishes, the displacement of death wishes, and the development of a concept of death from a reversible to an irreversible state. This is a well written, seminal paper, and it is interesting to note that modern day descriptions have not added much more.

Lourie (1966) described some further aspects of death concepts. In considering aspects of normal development, he observed that starting at the end of the first year of life the infant responds to separation, which may indicate that an equation is made between the *absence* and the *nonexistence* of a person who is out of sight. If mother is absent, the concept that she does not exist would be equivalent to death. This is a simple conception of death as absence. However, in its simplicity, in the next step in the process, is the wonderful one of control. If mother is absent (i.e. dead), she can return, or she can be made to return. When angry, the infant can turn away or shut his eyes and thereby remove (kill) the person involved in his anger. The development of retaliatory fantasies can be observed. For example, when the infant has faced separation and anxiety with the painful disappearance (death), particularly of the mother, we observe that when she comes back it is not unusual for the infant to turn away from her. She can be made to disappear, i.e. killed, by the infant in retaliation for her disappearance. Implicit in this demonstration of control is that fact that with older infants the concept of non-existence (that is, death) is not permanent. The significant person, who does not exist when she is out of sight, most often reappears. When the mother responds to the infant's retaliatory control of turning away by being hurt and rejected, and in particular when this is repeated, the infant learns that retaliation exists.This is especially so when the process is repeated. It is something that can be controlled and it exerts power over others, especially those who have power over you. The infant has learned an important lesson about what can be accomplished by removing yourself.

At ages two to four a child's fantasy life is replete with magic, whereby wish and fantasy can cause "death" — that is, the temporary removal of any one who offends her or who is in her way. The toddler begins to have fears of her own death, as extensions of being hurt and from the normal fears of inanimate objects, animals, natural forces, and the dark. At this point death, which is still thought of as reversible, becomes associated in the child's mind with violence. Aggressive fantasies become prominent in the three- to four-year-old. At age three to six, death wishes against a loved one who may be in the child's way become pointed. She becomes more concerned with fears of her own death, which is represented by the activity of humans, or witches, monsters, ghosts, giants, robbers, robots, or beings from outer space. Thus, we see from Lourie's description how the child learns from her experience and development:

• What death means

• How it can be used defensively

• How it can be used to influence and manoeuvre others

• How it can be a device to relieve helplessness

• How it can be used as a means of achieving importance in the lives of others.

Gould (1965) described the development of the concept of death as the following:

• At ages four to six death is equated with reversible separation, departure, and sleep.

• At ages five to nine, it is conceived of more in terms of murder, violence, retribution, and retaliation.

• Only at ages nine to ten or later does the child acquire a causal explanation of death.

There is some opinion however that attributes the knowledge of the irreversibility of death to children as young as age three to five (Kofkin, 1979). Conversely, the persistence into adulthood of the concept that death is not final is a frequent finding: one study of 600 children and adolescents found that 15% to 25% of a 13- to 16-year-old age group held this view (McIntyre et al., 1972).

It is perhaps not surprising to note how frequent the awareness of death wishes towards the self are found in the school-age and the pubescent child. In one study, 70 of 100 children with emotional problems reported thoughts about or wishes for their own death, while in a control group of "normal" children, 50% had thoughts of killing themselves. In another study in response to the question, "Are there times when you wished that you were dead?", 40% of 600 children between the ages of five and 18 years replied "occasionally" and 3% said "frequently" (Sobel, 1970). As the concepts of death become more refined, the motivations for suicide seem to develop from the unpremeditated act of the younger child to the more internalized, conflict-resolving attempt of the older one (Shaffer, 1974).

Nagy (1948), in an investigation of beliefs of death among 378 children, noted that in general children younger than five did not recognize death as irreversible; those aged five to nine envisaged death as a person; and those older than nine recognized that it is a biological process. This study was important in showing how concepts of death changed with development. Of course, development is not a uniform process, and children of the same age can have differing concepts of death. This was illustrated in a study by Melear (1973), who demonstrated the importance of such factors as cognitive level, personal experience, and emotional state.

Pfeffer (1986) noted that suicidal children, in contrast to their peers, often have intense preoccupations with death and consider it to be reversible and pleasant. She suggests that an excess of preoccupation with death in any child, regardless of actual experiences, should be considered as a warning of the possibility of suicidal tendencies. In other studies, Pfeffer and her associates (1979, 1980, 1982, 1984) demonstrated that suicidal children have preoccupations with fears of their own death and with that of family members, experience dreams about people dying and fantasies of how they die, and that many believe that death is a temporary, pleasant state that will relieve all tensions.

Brent (1977) provided an excellent example of the concept of death as expressed by a two-year-old who awoke in the night screaming for a bottle. With some insightful questioning, it was determined that the child equated not obtaining the bottle with "running out of gas," "not making contact," "my engine won't go," and "my motor won't run and I'll die."

Speec and Brent (1984) surveyed the literature on cognitive development in relationship to children's concept of death, noting that young children have a good grasp of death and its meaning. They described how this concept and the comprehension of it widens and deepens with age. Kane (1978, 1979) noted that at age three there was only a slight awareness of death; by five death was perceived as a condition of immobility and separation; at six the concepts of irreversibility, causality, lack of bodily functions and universality were acquired; by eight, death was perceived as the nonfunctioning of the senses; and by the age of 12, there was clear understanding of the distinction between the dead and the living.

Studies conducted by Orbach and colleagues (Orbach, Gross et al., 1985; Orbach, Talmon, et al., 1985) looked at five concepts of death—old age, universality, finality, causality, and irreversibility, as assessed with an objective questionnaire. Children were analyzed within three age groups: six to seven, eight to nine, and ten to eleven, and intelligence was rated. The younger children found causality the most difficult concept to understand, and they had trouble with finality as well. The concepts of finality, irreversibility, universality, and old age were incorporated almost simultaneously by the seven- and eight-year-olds, but a grasp of causality arose only among those aged ten and eleven. Intelligence influenced the child's ability to understand almost all of the concepts listed, with the only exception being causality. It is interesting to note that both Kane and Orbach indicated that very young children can have a quite realistic perception of death, including the concepts of its finality and irreversibility.

Piaget's structural theory of cognitive development offers another useful perspective on this question. Piagetian psychologists claim that from birth to two, the age of the sensorimotor period, there is definitely no awareness of death and no comprehension of it (although this is contrary to clinical evidence). During the preoperational stage of two to seven, with the initial acquisition of language and symbolic thought a broader conception of death is allowed: however, this is distorted by aspects of egocentricity, concrete thinking, and magical thinking. Here, death is often seen as a temporary and reversible condition. At age seven to twelve, characterized by Piaget as the concrete operational stage of cognitive development when the child begins to apply logic to solving problems, death begins to be perceived as a finality: however, it is not seen as universal or as a personal phenomenon. With the arrival of the abstract operational stage at age twelve and above, children apparently have reached completely mature levels and thought becomes abstract, logical, hypothetical, and objective. Death then assumes an adult definition as being biologically irreversible and a personal event.

Psychodynamics

Suicide, like most behaviors, is determined at the same time by many factors and represents the end-point of an inner and outer personal complexity. A suicidal attempt must be understood in reference as to whether or not there were any premonitory signs indicating its imminent approach. If so, knowledge of their existence might help prevent an actual suicide (see Chapter 5 on treatment and prevention). However, up to the present day there has been a complete lack of agreement about the existence of such symptoms (Lukianowicz, 1968). We will consider manifestations of risk factors more closely in Chapter 4.

When we look at what events may precipitate suicidal attempts, we find that almost anything is possible. This question is further complicated by the fact that the consciously given reason may not be related to the underlying, unconscious dynamic factor (Gould, 1965). Precipitating events are described as varying from seemingly minor rebuffs to severe circumstances such as separation, loss, or the death of a parent. One report (Kofkin, 1979) indicated that the most common trigger appeared to be an acute conflict between the child and the parental figures, with the attempts of younger children often reported to follow some slight or rejection that may seem minor or unimportant to the adult. The common underlying theme to a myriad of precipitating events seems to be rejection and deprivation, which results from the loss of love and support (Gould, 1965). One study reported that 76 percent of a group of suicides had experienced a significant loss, separation, or the anniversary of such a loss within days or weeks of their deaths. These losses and separations included death, illness, and hospitalization (Morrison & Collier, 1969). Separation by divorce or death is found in one third of all suicide attempters (Ackerley, 1967). In consideration of the multiple determinants of self-destructive behavior in children and adolescents, various authors, well aware of the blending of the external stress factors and internal conflicts, have attempted to group primary motivating factors. For example, Mattson and colleagues (1969) described six such groups:

- Group 1: Loss of a love object followed by acute or prolonged grief. These patients had sustained the death of or desertion by a parent or peer of the opposite sex. They were overtly depressed and stated their wish to die and join the deceased person. There existed a pervasive sense of loneliness and despair, which was more characteristic than guilt or self-depreciation.

- Group 2: "Bad me," markedly self-depreciating patients. These were boys (especially younger ones) who were prominent in expressing in-ward hostility and a loss of a sense of well-being. It was characteristic of these children to state in effect, "I'm good for nothing and must die."

- Group 3: The final "cry for help" directed beyond the immediate family. Girls predominated in this group, and the primary factor was overwhelming external stress. Family chaos, material scarcity, and physical illness had been present for a considerable period of time.

- Group 4: The revengeful, angry teenager. These adolescents clearly stated the manipulative aspects of their suicidal gestures ("This will teach Dad a lesson!"). They denied any serious intent, and frequently would also make homicidal threats when angry.

- Group 5: The psychotic adolescent. These patients appeared to regard suicide more as a desperate means to relieve increasing tension and confusion. Repeated threats were more common.

- Group 6: The "suicidal game." For these adolescents, flirting with death was thrilling and the reaction of their stunned peers were rewarding.

With regard to this last group, many of us have met teenagers whose existence as a feeling — therefore, alive — human being depended on such intense excitement that they would perform death-defying behavior in order to achieve it. For example, I treated one boy who was in the habit of leaping down in front of a rapidly approaching subway train and scrambling up the other side of the platform, just narrowly avoiding being hit. This would not only thrill his peers, but provide him with a sense of intense excitement that would make him "feel alive."

A somewhat different dynamic-causal grouping of patients was described by Gould (1965) with a basic formulation that stressed the importance of rejection and deprivation. The respective suicidal motivations of these groups were:

- Group 1: The wish to gain support and strength through joining the lost loved object (e.g., reuniting with a dead parent).

- Group 2: Retaliation for abandonment. If faced or threatened with rejection or abandonment, the youngster may say, "You can't leave me, I'm leaving you." Punishment of the other person, as well as a demonstration of power and control to mask feelings of helplessness, are in evidence.

- Group 3: Manipulation and blackmail to obtain love and attention and to punish others. ("You'll be sorry when I'm dead; you should treat me better. If you want me alive, pay attention to me and show me that you care.")

- Group 4: Atonement for one's sins by dying.

- Group 5: Self-murder, where the anger against another is of great intensity but cannot be expressed outwardly. This anger is turned inward and symbolically represents the murder of someone else.

- Group 6: Disintegration of the personality, in the course of an active psychotic process.

• Group 7: A last cry for help — a metaphorical S.O.S. sent out when the child feels overwhelmed.

Much earlier, Toolan (1962) similarly listed categories of suicidal psychodynamics as:

• Internalized anger

• Manipulative attempts to gain love and attention or to punish another

• A signal of distress

• A reaction to feelings of inner disintegration

• A desire to join a dead relative.

Other articles repeatedly stress factors of aggression such as revenge or spite ("You'll be sorry when I'm gone!") or turning of the aggression against oneself. An escape from an intolerable situation or reality is another major theme (Lourie, 1966). The escape motif is frequently mentioned (Kofkin, 1979).

Ackerley (1967) defended a view that children who only threaten to kill themselves and those who actually attempt to do so exhibited certain critical differences, as opposed to merely representing points on a continuum. This hypothesis holds that those children who have made a serious actual attempt in self-destruction show a widespread regression in ego function and a rupture in total ego integrity, i.e., a major break in reality, with marked despair and hopelessness.

There has been some emphasis placed on the function of suicide as a communication within the family — the "cry for help" aspect (Morrison & Collier, 1969). This has been conceptualized as an attempt at communication; as more than an impulsive act. This communication occurs as the culmination of growing conflict; and as a last resort. Suicide in

this conceptualization was seen as a symptom of an underlying disruption, more carefully described as various forms
of threatened or actual separation. Also from the perspective
of family pathology, it was suggested that in some instances
suicide represents a specific communication that derives from
living in a subculture (i.e., the family) where suicidal behavior
is a recognized form of communication. In such families one
hears much talk about suicide and death, and there may have
been untreated suicidal attempts. A kind of suicidal "modeling"
has been postulated (Kofkin, 1979; Kreitmann, 1970; Shaffer,
1974).

Shaffer described two "personality stereotypes" as evolv-
ing from his very important study:

1) Children who, although they had one or more friends at
   school, seemed to lead a solitary, isolated existence. They
   were of superior intelligence and seemed culturally distinct
   from their parents, who were less well educated. Their
   mothers were mentally ill. The reason for these children's
   suicides was not explicit. Before their deaths they had
   appeared depressed or withdrawn. They may have been
   absent from   school.

2) Children, including a few girls, who were judged to be
   impetuous and prone to aggressive or violent outbursts, to
   be unduly suspicious, and sensitive to and resentful of
   criticism. They had frequently been in trouble at school.

As emphasized earlier, depression has been reported to
be an important causal factor. Gould (1965) was one of the
early authors to defend the view that depression was a common
state in children and adolescents, one that was often overlooked, and almost always a part of the underlying psychodynamics of suicide.

Stressing the importance of the view for prevention, Shaffer
enumerated a high rate of typical symptoms of depression

for weeks preceding the self-destructive act. In 1974 Shaffer also listed a number of other factors apparent in a child's death by suicide. These include:

- A degree of conceptual maturity

- A disturbed family background

- A depressed mental state

- A precipitating incident often of a humiliating kind

- Access to the means of suicide and the opportunity to use it in isolation

- Close experience of suicidal behavior, either through its occurrence in the family or within a peer group or at a fantasy level.

Assessment

In reviewing aspects of the assessment of suicide in this age group, it is important to know the factors of high risk well. These include certain non-specific factors such as the imitation effect, wherein a statistically significant relationship has been established between media coverage of a suicide and temporarily associated increases in adolescent suicidal behaviors (Gould & Shaffer, 1986; Phillips, 1974; Phillips & Carstenson, 1986). This effect has been demonstrated with general information or feature stories on television, with fictional television movies, with novels and poems about suicide, and with newspaper reports. The increase in the rate of imitative suicidal behavior is directly proportional to the fame and attractiveness of the person who died and to the prominence of the news coverage. These findings require replication with larger sample sizes, as do Gould and Shaffer's (1986) finding that providing a comprehensive prevention program (including hotlines during and after the movie and study guides sent to schools) for one broadcast resulted in no increase in rate of suicidal behavior as compared with three other broadcasts.

More importantly, various specific factors should be known. These include the following:

• Medico-psychiatric symptoms — past and present

• Previous suicidal behavior

• Family history of psychiatric illness

• Family functioning factors

    - family discord and breakdown

    - parental employment factors

    - child abuse

• Scholastic achievement.

In deriving this list, the so-called "medico-psychiatric" and "statistical-social" models have been incorporated. This allows for the study of all high risk factors, and facilitates the development of management initiatives.

The factors listed here are to a large extent self-explanatory. In terms of medico-psychiatric symptoms, the presence of a chronic physical illness or hypochondriacal preoccupations with illness are important factors in suicide: Garfinkel and Golombek (1983) have shown that as many as 51% of adolescents attempting suicide suffer from medical problems. Adam (1983) has reported that the incidence of psychiatric disorder in suicide completers in North American ranges from 50-90%. Psychiatrically disordered children and adolescents present a much higher risk in terms of the full range of suicidal behavior than does the age-equivalent general population. The most prevalent disorders associated with suicidal behavior include conduct disorder, depressive disorders (including adjustment disorders with depressed mood, dysthymic disorders, and major affective disorders), drug and alcohol disorders, and psychotic disorders. There is also a consensus in the research literature that 50-75% of adolescents exhibiting the full range of suicidal behavior have demonstrated features of depression in the preceding month. In adult populations there are ongoing research studies attempting to identify biological markers that are correlates of suicide. Currently, the serotonergic data seem the most compelling — that low or declining cerebrospinal fluid concentrations of 5-hydroxy indole acetic acid (5-HIAA) in suicide attempters predict a poor prognosis (Shaffer et al., 1988).

Past suicidal behavior begets future suicidal behavior. In adolescents, researchers have demonstrated repetition rates that vary between 8% and 60%, with the Ontario Child Health Study (see Chapter 1) having a 36% rate. Shaffer (1974), in studying the records of children committing suicide over an eight-year period in England and Wales noted that 40% had demonstrated previous suicidal behavior.

There is a well documented high rate of both psychiatric disorder and suicidal behavior in the families of suicidal youth. Garfinkel and Golombek (1983) found psychiatric illness in 62% of families in the suicidal group versus 16% in the families of the control group. A history of suicidal behavior or completed suicide was seven times higher in the first group.

Family functioning factors are also implicated as a factor in suicidal behavior, with the lack of a supportive family network considered to be a causative factor (Shaffer, 1974). Several studies have replicated these findings regarding family discord and breakdown. Garfinkel and Golombek (1983) found parental separation or death three times as often in the suicide attempter group than in the control group, divorce twice as often, absent father 50% versus 14%, more than half of the single mothers working outside the home, and placement outside the home eight times more often. The father's unemployment was also a factor. Child abuse and neglect are implicated as well: Rosenthal and Rosenthal (1984) demonstrated a higher prevalence of child abuse and neglect in their group of suicidal preschoolers, compared with a behavior disordered control group. Green (1978), in a small unitary study, demonstrated that 40% of abused children later exhibit a life-threatening behavior.

We emphasize here that an evaluation of the presenting problem, history of the presenting problem, and other relevant background information is necessary. One must assess the previously mentioned high risk factors, explore any verbal and behavioral warning signals, and carefully evaluate mental status, including a focus on the suicidal component (Voineskos & Lowy, 1985). The method of choice of suicide attempt and its lethality needs to be seriously evaluated, as well as evaluation of the family system and the support network. Corroboration from family and friends is necessary.

Assessment of suicidal potential should include the following points (Voineskos & Lowy, 1985): Take all attempts or threats seriously. Perform a complete psychiatric evaluation. Ask about suicidal intent and plans. Ask about the consequences of suicide to the family, friends, etc. Discuss alternate solutions. Interview the "significant others" (family, friends).

In addition, the characteristics suggestive of serious suicidal intent must be noted, including an assessment of the following aspects (Beck et al., 1974): Was it carried out in isolation? Was it timed so that intervention was unlikely? Were precautions taken to avoid discovery? Were preparations made in anticipation of death? Were other people informed beforehand of the individual's intention? Was there evidence of extensive premeditation? Was a suicide note left? Were other people alerted following the attempt?

The involvement of the family and significant others is essential both in terms of the assessment and to initiate the treatment process. This is accomplished by developing a beginning therapeutic alliance, and by limiting denial and the minimization of the suicidal act. An effort is made to help the family cope with the feelings of shame, disbelief, and social disapproval. As well, the family in crisis is considerably more workable and amenable to exploring adaptive systemic changes that might reduce suicidal potential (Davidson, in press). Similar beginning treatment initiatives apply to the patient. As Eisenberg (1980) observed, "What is crucial is a therapeutic context that permits the rebuilding of hope and the reestablishment of healthy ties among family members. Because the patient feels unloved and unworthy of love, the task of treatment is to convey a sense of caring and to restore faith in the possibility of a satisfying future."

Scholastic difficulties can be either the cause or the result of psycho-pathology in suicidal behavior, with several studies demonstrating an associated 35-75% failure or drop-out rate. However, others have revealed no differences between a suicidal group and a control group.

Because of the significant factor of under-reporting of suicide attempts, in cases of treatment of apparent accidents in pediatric emergency rooms the clinician must at least be suspicious under certain conditions. These conditions would include, for example, an "accidental" overdose by medication in a depressed youngster. Too often such patients are not questioned carefully, nor are other possible sources of information such as parents or peers properly interviewed. Unlike the case where the patient presents after a documented or observed suicide attempt, it is hard to assess imminent or potential risk if suicidal motivation is not even being considered a possibility. (Of course, it is even easier to establish the occurrence of a suicide after its successful completion: however, that is what all clinicians are attempting to avoid.) Therefore, the suspicion of suicide must be heightened to become part of the consciousness of the clinician in his or her daily work.

Once the clinician's suspicions are raised, then the manifestations of suicidal risk factors, such as depressive symptomatology or the presence of hopelessness, humiliation, and impulsivity, can be looked for in the proper conduct of a careful psychiatric and psychosocial history. As reviewed in Chapter 4, there are a variety of manifestations of risk factors, which can be defined along a spectrum ranging from suicidal ideation, to suicidal threats, to suicidal attempts, to completed suicide. One has to estimate the intensity of the variety of factors known to correlate directly with suicidal tendencies, such as the availability of firearms. The assessment of intentionality and of lethality are also important. There are a variety of classes of risk factors, including depression, pessimism, hopelessness, impulsivity, and conduct disorders. The patient's sense of basic worthwhileness or its loss should be assessed. A variety of developmental experiences such as an early severe psycho-social trauma or the presence of child abuse can increase the risk, and these should be inquired after.

When confronted with a youth who has already attempted suicide, the measurement or estimation of the future risk can proceed with greater efficacy. The establishment of the existence of depression, its severity, the presence of a conduct disorder, and substance abuse are all factors that can be looked at carefully and used in making these estimations. Such manifestations of risk will be reviewed in Chapter 4. A good conceptual understanding of all of these manifestations and of the various groupings of risk factors is imperative for the clinician's armamentarium, as is a thorough knowledge of the diagnostic criteria for depressive disorders, major depressive disorders, dysthymia and cyclothymia according to DSM-III-R criteria.

As with adults, the suicidal attempt should be carefully reviewed in terms of its lethality. The majority of successful suicides among adolescents are committed with firearms; therefore, the use of a firearm in the attempt or the ready availability of firearms in the youth's immediate environment becomes an important factor of risk to note. The usual questions that one asks an adult about a suicidal attempt should also be asked here, such as whether the individual was alone or with another person at the time the attempt took place. In the context of the family, was the attempt manifestly a form of communication (the famous "cry for help") or was it a more lethal, solitary break in communication? Was the attempt discovered only by chance?

All of these factors have to be discussed with the patient and his or her family. In addition, any other ancillary sources of information such as the child's peer group or his/her school performance are important. The slow, careful, proper conduct of a complete psychiatric, psychological and social history with the consideration of suicide as a possible risk is emphasized. Just as the diagnosis of depression depends on a proper investigation (see Chapter 3), one has to acknowledge the existence of suicide and its marked incidence in our society and must then pay recognition to this incidence through proper clinical assessment.

In keeping with our understanding of the range of suicidal behaviors, from ideas of self-destruction to threats of suicidal acts to actual acts, clinical questioning of a patient must take into account this range of behavior. All of these questions would be included in a proper history and mental status examination. As will be discussed further in this book, all of the important manifestations of a suicidal episode in children and adolescents can be described according to its motivation, its duration, its method of enactment, its lethality, its intent for self-harm, and the potential to abort the act. Each must be carefully understood and recognized by any clinician working with children.

Recommended Reading

Pfeffer, C. R. (1986). *The suicidal child.* New York: Guilford Press.

An excellent book that reviews research data and the clinical spectrum of suicide in this age group with depth and understanding.

Shaffer, D. (1974). Suicide in childhood and early adolescence. *Journal of Child Psychology and Psychiatry, 15,* 275-291.

A classic epidemiological study.

Hug-Hellmuth, H. (1912). The child's concept of death. Translated by Ernst Kris. *Psychoanalytic Quarterly, 34,* 499-516.

One of the first papers ever written on this topic.

1) Orbach, I., Gross, Y., Glaubman, H., & Berman, D. (1985). Children's perception of death in humans and animals as a function of age, anxiety and cognitive ability. *Journal of Child Psychology and Psychiatry, 26,* 453-463.
2) Orbach, I., Talmom, O., Kedem, P., & Harr Even, D. (1985). Sequential patterns of the death concepts in children. *Journal of the American Academy of Child Psychiatry, 26,* 578-582.

These two papers are the most up-to-date studies on the topic of the concept of death in children.

References

Ackerley, W. (1967). Latency age children who threaten or attempt to kill themselves. *Journal of the American Academy of Child Psychiatry, 6*, 242-261.

Adam, K. (1983). Suicide and attempted suicide. *Medicine North America, 3200-3207.*

Beck, A.T., Schuyler, R.D., & Herman, J. (1974). Development of suicidal intent scales. In A.T. Beck, H. Resnick, & D. Lettieri (Eds.), *The prediction of suicide.* Springfield, IL: Charles C. Thomas.

Brent, S.B. (1977). Puns, metaphors and misunderstanding in a 2-year-old's conception of death. *Omega, 8*, 285-295.

Davidson, Simon, I. (in press). Suicide. In L. Sheer (Ed.), *Death, dying, bereavement and loss.* London: Blackwell Scientific.

Eisenberg, L. (1980). Adolescent suicide: On taking arms against a sea of troubles. *Pediatrics, 66*, 315-320.

Garfinkel, B.D., & Golombek, H. (1983). Suicidal behavior in adolescents. In H. Golombek & B.D. Garfinkel (Eds.), *The adolescent and mood disturbance.* New York: International Universities Press.

Gould, R. (1965). Suicide problems in children and adolescents. *American Journal of Psychotherapy, 19*, 228-246.

Gould, M.S., & Shaffer, D. (1986). The impact of suicide on television movies: Evidence and imitation. *New England J. of Med., 315 (11)*, 690-694.

Green, A.H. (1978). Self-destructive behavior in battered children. *American Journal of Psychiatry, 135*, 579-582.

Hug-Hellmuth, H. (1912). The child's concept of death. Translated by Ernst Kris. *Psychoanalytic Quarterly, 34*, 499-516.

Kane, B. (1978). *Children's concept of death.* Unpublished doctoral dissertation, University of Cincinnati.

Kane, B. (1979). Children's conception of death. *Journal of Genetic Psychology, 134*, 141-153.

Kofkin, M. (1979). Suicide. In M. Josephson & R. Porter (Eds.), *Clinician's handbook of childhood psychopathology.* New York: Jason Aronson.

Kreitmann, N . (1970). Attempted suicide as language: An empirical study. *British Journal of Psychiatry, 116,* 465-473

Lourie, R. (1966). Clinical studies of attempted suicide. *Clinical Proceedings of the Children's Hospital, 22,* 163-173.

Mattson, A., Seese, L., & Hawkins, J. (1969). Suicidal behavior as a child psychiatric emergency. *Archives of General Psychiatry, 20,* 100-109.

McIntyre, M., & Angle, C. (1970). Taxonomy of suicide as seen in poison control centres. *Paediatric Clinics of North America, 17,* 697-706.

McIntyre, M., Angle, C., & Struempler, L. (1972). The concept of death in mid-western children and youth. *American Journal of Disease of Children, 123,* 527-532.

Melear, J. (1973). Childrens' conception of death. *Journal of Genetic Psychology, 123,* 359-360.

Morrison, G., & Collier, J. (1969). Family treatment approaches to suicidal children and adolescents. *Journal of the American Academy of Child Psychiatry, 8,* 140-153.

Nagy, M. (1948). The child's view of death. *Journal of Genetic Psychology, 73,* 3-27.

Orbach, I., Gross, Y., Glaubman, H., & Berman, D. (1985) Children's perception of death in humans and animals as a function of age, anxiety and cognitive ability. *Journal of Child Psychology and Psychiatry, 26,* 453-463.

Orbach, I., Talmom, O., Kedem, P., & Harr Even, D. (1985). Sequential patterns of the death concepts in children. *Journal of the American Academy of Child Psychiatry, 26,* 578-582.

Pfeffer, C. R. (1986). *The suicidal child.* New York: Guilford Press.

Pfeffer, C. R., Conte, H.R., Plutcjik, R. and Jerrett, J. (1979). Suicidal behavior in latency-age children: An empirical study. *Journal of the American Academy of Child Psychiatry, 18,* 679-692.

Pfeffer, C.R., Conte, H.R., Plutcchik, R. and Jerrett, J. (1980). Suicidal behavior in latency-age children: An empirical study: An outpatient population. *Journal of the American Academy of Child Psychiatry*, 19, 703-710.

Pfeffer, C.R., Soloman, G., Plutchik, R., Mizruchi, M.S. and Weiner, A.(1982) Suicidal behavior in latency-age in-patients: A replication and cross-validation. *Journal of the American Academy of Child Psychiatry*, 21, 564-569.

Pfeffer, C.R., Zucherman, S., Plutchik, R. and Mitzruchi, M.S. (1984). Suicidal behavior in normal school children: A comparison with child psychiatric inpatients. *Journal of the American Academy of Child Psychiatry*, 23, 416-423.

Phillips, D.P. (1974). The influence of suggestion on suicide: Substantive and theoretical implication of the Werther Effect. *Am. Social Rev., 39,* 340-354.

Phillips, D.P., & Carstenson, L.L. (1986). Clustering of teenage suicide after television news stories about suicide. *New England J. of Med., 315 (11),* 685-689.

Rosenthal, A.P., & Rosenthal, S. (1984). Suicidal behavior by preschool children. *Am. J. Psychiatry, 141,* 4.

Shaffer, D. (1974). Suicide in childhood and early adolescence. *J. of Child Psychology and Psychiatry, 15,* 275-291.

Shaffer, D., Garland, A., Gould, M., Fisher, P., & Trautman, P. (1988). Preventing teenage suicide: A critical review. *J. Am. Acad. Child Adolesc. Psychiatry, 27 (6),* 675-687.

Speec, M.W., & Brent, S.B. (1984). Children's understanding of death: A review of three components of the death concept. *Child Development, 55,* 1671-1686.

Toolan, J. (1962). Suicide and suicidal attempts in children and adolescents. *American Journal of Psychiatry, 118,* 719-724.

Voineskos, G., & Lowy, F.H. (1985). Suicide and attempted suicide. In S.E. Greben, V.M. Rakoff, & G. Voineskos (Eds.), *A method of psychiatry.* Philadelphia: Lea and Febiger.

Chapter 3

Depressive Disorders in Children and Adolescents

George MacLean, M.D.

Although children have been treated for depressive disorders for decades, it is only in recent years that definitive diagnoses have been made. Prior to this, the actual existence of depression in this age group was debated. There was a lack of uniform opinion about a careful definition of reliable, defined diagnostic criteria to enable a proper diagnosis or a classification of the disorder; therefore it was overlooked or its existence even denied. Considerable debate existed around the proper appreciation of depression as a normal variation of a mood or even as a symptom, and particularly as a definite psychopathological syndrome. The occurrence of depression in children was questioned by some from the experientially distant viewpoint of metapsychology, who argued in a rarefied manner that depression was an impossibility because a child did not have a fully developed superego. The faulty logic in such an argument was countered by the clinical experience of empirically interested child analysts, psychiatrists, and others, who were seeing more and more depressed children in the consultation rooms of their daily practices. (Once again, it is interesting to note how one can see what one can see when one's point of view is not obstructed by theory, but aided by clinical experience from which theory is derived.)

Articles on child depression often refer to the classic papers of René Spitz on the withdrawal of children in emotionally cold institutional environments. Spitz (1945, 1946) described his basic findings in articles entitled "Hospitalism: The Inquiry into the Genesis of Psychiatric Conditions in Early Childhood" in the first volume of *The Psychoanalytic Study of the Child.* He defined hospitalism as "a vitiated condition of the body due to the long confinement in a hospital, or the morbid condition of the atmosphere of the hospital." However, he added, "to this symptomatology, it should be added the physiognomic expression in these cases is difficult to describe. This expression would be, in an adult, described as depression . . . . The syndrome in question is extremely similar to what is familiar to us from Abraham's and Freud's classic description of mourning, and melancholia. The factor which appears to be of decisive etiological significance in our cases is the loss of the love object . . . [it] comes closest to what Fenichel described pre-oedipal infantile depression, called by Abraham 'primal papathymia'."

Herbert Rie (1966) examined the applicability of "depression" to children and concluded that "the fully differentiated and generalized primary affect characterizing depression, namely despair or hopelessness, is one which children—perhaps prior to the end of latency years—are incapable." He complained that "the failure to specify the criteria for the diagnosis is keenly felt when the known symptoms differ grossly from those of adult depression. The diagnosis is announced but one is forced to confess that the term 'depression' has no familiar referent in child psychopathology."

Bowlby (1969) argued that ethological concepts, in particular "attachment," were better suited to organize observational data; stating that "the child's tie is best conceived as the outcome of a number of instinctual response systems, mostly non-oral in character, which are part of the inherited behavior repertoire of man: when they are activated and the mother figure is available, attachment behavior results." Bowlby attacked "the loyalty to the theory of infantile narcissism which remains a feature of the work of many leading analysts" as being responsible for the inadequate emphasis on the significance of psychopathology of grief and mourning in early childhood. To Bowlby, such concepts better clarified depression. (Bowlby, 1980)

In a very thorough and scholarly review by E. James Anthony (1975), the concept of childhood depression, its definition, its usage, its role in bereavement, its place as an emergent phenomenon of our time, and the psychoanalytic perspective are all described in detail. This excellent review is recommended to every reader in the area.

Current opinion has established that depression does indeed occur among children and adolescents, and there is ample support in the literature for the validity of such diagnoses. In modern classification, this is true for mood disorders of a major depressive type, cyclothymia, and dysthymia. The presence of bipolar disorders (manic or hypomanic) is much less frequent in younger children, occurring more often in adolescents. These will be described here only briefly.

Because of the wealth of experience derived from empirical work, by the time of the revision of the third edition of the *Diagnostic and Statistical Manual of Mental Disorders* (APA, 1987), it was the opinion that the essential features of mood disorders were the same in all age groups, and therefore that the diagnostic criteria for adults would apply to children and adolescents as well. Therefore, if a youngster presented with an illness that met the DSM-III-R criteria for either major depression, dysthymia, or cyclothymia, that diagnosis would be given.

However, although the common opinion now appears to be that depression in children, adolescents, and adults is similar if not the same, we must pay some respect to developmental differences. For example, there is some indication that depressive symptoms increase with age, and that the apparently equal epidemiological incidence between males and females among prepubertal age groups shifts to a much higher rate of females to males in adolescence and early adulthood (Angold, 1988).

Major depressive disorders do exist in childhood, and although they are rare they are very serious when they occur (Kovacs et al., 1984a, b). Kashani and Carlson (1987), studying seriously depressed preschoolers, noted a frequent association with physical or sexual abuse. Further study is needed to differentiate more correctly between the depressive symptomatology that is observed in prepubertal children and that among adolescents and adults.

In summary, it is interesting to follow the debate through the literature to its present state, where depression in children and adolescents is enshrined in DSM-III-R as a diagnostically valid condition. Spitz (1946) described an "anaclitic" depression, which he accounted for by the noted loss of a love object. This is different from the Kleinian concept of the "depressive position," a normal concept in that metapsychology. We have noted Bowlby's ethological theories of "attachment," and the denial of the existence of depression in children in the rather dogmatic paper by Herbert Rie (1966). Numerous papers appeared in the early 1970s that led to the condensation of the opinion stated in DSM-III-R. This opinion has been supported by an increased interest in the need for a careful and thorough assessment of children for depressive disorders.

Depression and the Link
With Suicide

In acknowledging the existence and the need for thorough assessment of depressive disorders, we must also look at the need for assessing them as a factor in the incidence of suicidal behavior. It is important to recognize the link between these two problems, as the association between them in children has been amply demonstrated. For example, Mattsson, Seese, and Hawkins (1969) discovered that among children referred to an emergency room service, 40% had exhibited signs of depression for at least one month before admission. In another important study, Shaffer (1974) reported that 32% of 31 children who had killed themselves had shown signs of depressed mood and tearfulness.

Proceeding from that definitive indication, Pfeffer and her colleagues (1979, 1980, 1982) have studied a number of different pediatric psychiatric populations and found that depression was correlated significantly with a broad display of suicidal ideation and behavior. In keeping with these findings, it was noted (Pfeffer et al., 1984) that depression was more severe among suicidal children than among nonsuicidal children in a sample of 10 schoolchildren.

Carlson and Cantwell (1982) interviewed 102 child and adolescent psychiatric inpatients and outpatients, and assessed the relationship between their severity of depression and the degree of suicidal ideas and attempts. Forty-five children had no suicidal ideas, 45 had occasional ideas of it, and 12 felt seriously like killing themselves. Of the total group, 22 had made a suicidal attempt. Importantly, it was noted that the average degree of depression for those with occasional suicidal ideas was greater than for those with none, but less than for those with severe suicidal ideation: 33% of those with occasional suicidal thoughts and 83% of those with serious suicidal ideation were diagnosed as having a major affective disorder. This study concluded that there was a direct relationship between feeling depressed and being suicidal. Further, there was a clear relationship between depression and suicidal ideation; clearer than that between depression and suicide attempts. It was also noted that not all children who were suicidal were depressed.

Robbins and Alessi (1985) evaluated associations between psychiatric symptoms and suicidal behavior in 64 adolescent inpatients using structured interviews. Subsequent statistical analysis indicated that there was a significant relationship between the symptoms of depressive disorders and suicidal risk. Symptoms that were associated with suicidal behavior included depressed mood, negative self-evaluation, anhedonia, insomnia, poor concentration, indecisiveness, lack of reactivity of mood, psychomotor disturbance, and alcohol and drug abuse.

An important study by Cohen-Sandler and colleagues (1982) further differentiated between depressed suicidal children and depressed nonsuicidal children, in that the former were experiencing increasing amounts of stress during maturation compared with other children in the study. This stress involved disruptive family events, such as losses and separations from important others.

From these various studies, it can be seen that depression is closely associated with suicidal behavior. The need for the clinician to know as much as possible about depression in this age group is therefore obvious. Any clinician encountering children in psychiatric emergencies, working with families, or in any form of pediatric practice would be confronted with depressed children almost constantly; thus, the ability to assess this disorder and further, to be aware of the risk of suicide and to be able to assess its severity, is very important.

In a large study of hospitalized preadolescent children, Kathleen Myers and her co-workers (1984) demonstrated that depression was highly correlated with suicidal behavior. As we have noted, other studies have found a relationship between depressive affect or syndrome and suicidal behaviors. However, these reports did not indicate as strong a relationship as was noted by Myers.

Carlson and Cantwell (1982) described two groups of suicidal children and adolescents. One group was depressed and the other group was behavior disordered. The strong association of depression with suicidal activity was important. There was a suggestion that the depressive and the conduct-disordered children were at greater risk of developing into affectively disordered and personality disordered adults, respectively (Myers et al., 1984). In a well designed study of depressive syndromes in children by Handford and colleagues (1986), it was noted that one common indicator of serious depression was suicidal ideation.

A major study by Brent and colleagues (1986) further showed that suicidal ideation and behavior were most significantly correlated with the various components of depression. That is, the various aspects of depression were the most significant correlates of suicidal ideation and behavior. Brent noted that these findings were similar to those of Pfeffer et al. (1979). Those children with a history of suicide attempts were more likely to show both the symptoms and the syndrome of depression.

An interesting relationship between the medical lethality of suicidal behavior and affective disorder has been noted in a study by David Brent (1987), who emphasized the important contribution of hopeless dysphoria. This study was consistent with other work that correlated the lethality of suicide attempts in children and adolescents with depression, as well as with factors such as being male, having suicidal intent, and a family history of depressive disorder. These variables have also been associated with the greatest risk of completed suicide (Otto, 1972; Shaffer, 1974; Welner et al., 1979). In a critical review of the prevention of teenage suicide, Shaffer and his colleagues (1988) noted that depressive illness was a specific individual predisposition to suicide.

In a study attempting to relate psychopathology to suicidal ideation in children and adolescents, Brent et al. (1986) noted that those with a history of suicidal attempts were more likely to show both the symptoms and the syndrome of depression. They felt that depression played a larger role in youthful suicidal behavior than hitherto had been realized. However, from the results of their study the findings could be attributed to the fact that their sample was a peculiar psychiatrically referred group. Yet, the suggestion that suicidal ideation and behavior were a continuous phenomena, was there.

Valez and Cohen (1988), in a study of 752 randomly selected children, reported that suicide attempters had 18 times the risk of a major depression than non-attempters and frequently experienced other serious consequences of their depression. Mothers of these children also reported experiencing more emotional and behaviorial problems with them and were more likely to have sought psychological help for them. Valez and Cohen concluded that the information regarding risk factors is of importance in understanding the origins of clinically identified suicide attempts, and emphasized the importance of depressive symptomatology in the history of suicide attempters. This finding has been reported in other clinical or otherwise treated populations, where it has been shown that children who have attempted suicide tend to have higher rates of depressive symptoms or diagnoses of depression than those children who have been treated for other conditions (Haler & Stansfeld, 1984; Otto, 1972; Pfeffer, 1981; Triolo-Santo et al., 1984).

Often there is a relationship between depression and conduct disorder. In a study by Marriage et al. (1986) of 60 children and adolescents referred for assessment of depression, 11 cases were found that met diagnostic criteria for both conduct disorder and affective disorder. Psychiatric ratings also indicated that the depressive symptoms were much more severe in cases of conduct disorder with depression than in cases of dysthymic disorder.

Poznanski et al. (1984) noted that one particular rating scale, the Children's Depression Rating Scale - Revised version (CDRS-R) was a reliable clinician-rated scale that differentiated the depressed from the nondepressed child. It seemed to provide a better estimate of depressive symptomatology than did clinical impressions.

Hoberman and Garfinkel (1988) reported from a sample of completed suicide in children and adolescents that these individuals were more likely to be older males with a current psychiatric disorder, usually an affective disorder or alcohol or drug abuse. Results of this study were similar to the previous study by Garfinkel and Golombek (1983), who identified significant psychiatric conditions in 25% of their sample, mostly depression. In addition, Shaffer (1974) found that significantly fewer of his subjects did not show affective or antisocial symptoms. Shaffer et al. (1988) demonstrated high rates of several psychiatric disorders in his sample: for example, 76% were depressed, 70% were alcohol or substance abusers, and 70% had symptoms of antisocial behavior.

In addition to ratings and interviews of the child and parents, extrafamilial sources of information may offer crucial information in determining the presence of a depressed mood and of an affective disorder.

Among those adolescents who attempt suicide, the presence of both major depressive disorders and borderline personality disorders significantly increases the severity of suicidal behavior (Freedman et al., 1983). Features of affective disorders and/or antisocial symptomatology were identified among young adolescent suicide victims by Shaffer (1974). The clinical dilemma regarding psychological risk factors for youth suicide involves the clinician's ability to recognize the signs and symptoms that are associated with these factors and to appreciate their importance.

DSM-III-R Diagnoses

DSM-III-R (APA, 1987) defines a mood *syndrome* as only being either depressive or manic. A mood syndrome is a group of mood and associated symptoms that occur for a minimal duration of time. A major depressive syndrome is defined as a depressed mood or loss of interest of at least two weeks' duration, accompanied by several associated symptoms such as weight loss and difficulty concentrating. A mood *episode,* major depressive, manic or hypomanic, is a mood syndrome that is not due to a known organic factor and is not part of a non-mood psychotic disorder. A mood *disorder* is determined by the pattern of mood episodes. For example, a diagnosis of major depression is made when there has been one or more major depressive episodes, but no history of a manic or unequivocal hypomanic episode. (It is noted that manic or hypomanic episodes are very rare in childhood, and become more frequent in adolescence.) We will here discuss three disorders: the major depressive episode, cyclothymia, and dysthymia or depressive neurosis.

Major Depressive Episode

As described in DSM III-R, the essential feature of a major depressive episode is either a depressed mood (or in children and adolescents possibly an irritable mood), a loss of interest or pleasure in all or almost all activities, and other associated symptoms (listed below). The symptoms must represent a change from previous functioning, and must have been persistent for a least a two-week period, occurring nearly every day for most of the day. At least five of the following symptoms must be noted, of which one must be either a depressed mood or a loss of interest of pleasure:

- A depressed mood (or an irritable mood in children and adolescents) as indicated by subjective account or by observation by others.

- Apathy; a markedly diminished interest or pleasure in all or almost all activities, as indicated by subjective account or by observations by others.

- A decrease or increase in appetite, and significant weight loss or weight gain when not dieting (more than 5% of body weight in a month). In children, we must consider a failure to make expected weight gains during development.

- Insomnia or hypersomnia.

- Psychomotor agitation or retardation, observable by others and not merely subjective feelings of restlessness or of being slowed down.

- Fatigue or loss of energy.

- Feelings of worthlessness or excessive or inappropriate guilt which may be delusional, i.e., not merely self-reproach or guilt about being sick.

- Diminished ability to think or concentrate, or indecisiveness, again by either subjective account or as observed by others.

- Recurrent thoughts of death, and not just as a fear of dying. Recurrent suicidal ideation is noted without a specific plan. Finally, there can be a suicidal attempt or a specific plan for committing suicide.

This diagnosis is not made if an organic factor may have initiated and maintained the disturbance; if the disturbance is a normal reaction to the death of a loved one—that is, uncomplicated bereavement; if at any time during the disturbance there have been delusions or hallucinations; or if the disturbance is superimposed on schizophrenia, schizophreniform disorder, delusional disorder, or psychotic disorder.

As in other diagnostic disorders described in DSM-III-R, criteria for severity of the syndrome or episode are noted. These range from mild to moderate to severe, with or without psychotic features. In addition, there is accommodation made for whether or not the illness is in partial or in full remission. A full remission is defined as no significant signs or symptoms of the disturbance for the past six months.

Dysthymia, or Depressive Neurosis

The essential feature of this disorder in children and adolescents is a chronic disturbance involving a depressed or irritable mood, as indicated either by subjective account or by observation by others, along with some of the following associated symptoms:

• Poor appetite or overeating

• Insomnia or hypersomnia

• Low energy or fatigue

• Low self-esteem

• Poor concentration or difficulty making decisions

• Feelings of hopelessness

There must be at least a one-year period in which the individual is never without depressive symptoms for more than two months, and these symptoms are in evidence for most of the day for more days than not.

Dysthymia is frequently seen as a secondary type; that is, as a consequence of a pre-existing chronic, non-mood AXIS I or AXIS III disorder (for example, anorexia nervosa, somatization disorder, psychoactive substance dependence, an anxiety disorder, or rheumatoid arthritis). Cases that develop before the age of 21 are specified as early onset and those that develop after 21 as late onset. It is of note that some researchers believe the early onset primary type represents a distinct nosologic entity.

Particularly in young people, the boundary of dysthymia with major depression is unclear. Definitely, a quantitative judgment is in order. Because this disorder often begins in youth, it has often been referred to as a depressive personality. It usually begins without a clear onset and has a chronic course; impairment in social and occupational functioning is usually mild or moderate and exists because of the chronicity rather than the severity of the syndrome. Social interaction with peers and adults is frequently affected. Children with depression often react negatively or shyly to praise and frequently respond to positive relationships with negative behaviors. School performance and progress may be badly affected.

The diagnosis is not made if there is clear evidence of a major depressive episode during this period, if the disturbance is superimposed on a chronic psychotic disorder such as schizophrenia or delusional disorder, if it is sustained by specific organic factors or substances, or if there has ever been a manic or unequivocal hypomanic episode.

Cyclothymia

This chronic disorder of mood involves numerous hypomanic episodes and periods of depressed mood, or a loss of interest or pleasure of insufficient severity or duration to meet the criteria for a major depressive or manic episode. In order to make this diagnosis, there must be a one-year period in which the individual is never without hypomanic or depressive symptoms for more than two months. It is not made if there is clear evidence of a manic episode or a major depressive episode during the first two years of the disturbance. The boundaries between cyclothymia and a bipolar disorder are not well defined. This disorder usually begins in adolescence; it is rare in childhood. Diagnostic criteria for cyclothymia include:

- The presence of numerous hypomanic episodes and numerous periods of depressed mood or loss of interest or pleasure that do not meet the criteria of a major depressive episode.

- The patient is never free of hypomanic or depressive symptoms for more than two months at a time.

The diagnosis is not made if there is clear evidence of a major depressive disorder or manic episode during the first year. Care must be taken to distinguish between a cyclothymic disorder and the various bipolar disorders of a manic or a depressed type.

Assessment

At the present time there are three rapidly developing and maturing aspects of assessment in the area of depression among children and adolescents: clinical interviews of the child and of the parents, semistructured interviews, and rating scales.

Clinical Interviews

As child depression as a clinical disorder has become more and more apparent, more definitive attention has been paid to the clinical interview. It is generally accepted that direct examination is likely to provide valid data that can be applied according to accepted diagnostic criteria.

A long tradition exists of communication through play and verbal interchange. Some clinicians have expressed a concern that such communication is more directed at a delineation of psychodynamics than at the more definitive aspects of a clinical diagnosis, or that it represents a distraction. However, in the assessment of younger children, there is a contrary opinion that play and play techniques of interviewing remain an important element. It is vital to be able to communicate at a child's level of cognitive and verbal development, and it is only distracting if the interviewer does not have a clear concept of the goal of the interview—which is to carefully observe, assess, and make conclusions about the existence of criteria that indicate a depressive disorder.

Some clinicians do find it distracting to play, feeling obligated by the constraints of their own personalities to maintain a somewhat adultamorphic restraint in their clinical interchange. Those who feel freer to do so and at the same time can maintain an observational stance, can utilize a combination of play and verbal techniques (when age- and developmentally appropriate) in order to make a correct diagnosis. Play does not *negate* the necessity of asking very careful questions about the type and nature of any symptomatology present, but it can be used to interview children and to give them the opportunity to describe their symptoms and worries.

As in any interview situation, the ability to communicate and to obtain the child's trust is necessary in constructing a proper relationship. This will permit a dialogue to occur, the context of which the clinician's questions can be answered with great validity. It is often very enlightening to see a child welcome an interview: children do experience pain, and doctors often are very readily accepted in their role of relievers of pain. This cognitive view of the clinician as someone who attempts to understand problems and come to solutions is paramount. It can easily be determined how much a child understands of the situation and of the interviewer's role. Often children initially provide definitions given to them by their parents; however, with the proper dialogue they can quickly come to present their own understanding, and achieve a more correct appreciation of the existence of their problem and of the interviewer as a helper to deal with it. Certainly, this demands trust.

In the context of the individual interview, careful assessment of the symptoms should be attempted, including a general inquiry about depression. The nature of this depressive mood should be put carefully into the particular language of the child, as children use different words to express their feelings. Usually older ones can be more adult in their descriptions. As with adults, the nature of the depressed mood, its diurnal variation, and its reactivity to environmental events should be questioned and careful descriptions obtained. Careful respect should be paid to the child's concept of time, in determining the duration of symptoms.

In addition to the assessment of a presence of the depressed mood and its characteristic and nature, other areas of inquiry include the presence of changes in appetite or weight, school performance and difficulties in doing school work, fatigue or lack of energy, anxiety, suicidal ideation or behavior, and the possible lack of interest in all life events. All such symptomatology is questioned, and when possible the most careful description of any symptoms are obtained. The presence of any psychotic symptoms such as hallucinations or delusions must also be part of the general inquiry. As with adults they are congruent with a depressed mood.

In addition to taking a history with the child, an interview with the parents is of particular importance. This has valid descriptive ability in detecting children with psychiatric disorders. It is also important to take a careful psychiatric history and carry out a mental status examination of the parents themselves. Existence of depressive disorders within the family, most particularly the parents, is an important indicator and predictor of depression in the child. Historic events such as loss, bereavement, and deprivation are also vital to note, as such events again predict the presence of a depressive disorder.

Semistructured Interviews

The DSM-III-R diagnostic criteria described earlier are currently in wide use. Historically, criteria for the diagnosis of childhood depressive disorders originated from the Feighner Research Diagnostic Criteria in Adults (see Spitzer et al, 1978). Weinberg and colleagues (1973) had earlier described other criteria, but there is a general opinion that these were not especially definitive.

There was a need to refine the diagnosis of depression, both for clinical reasons and to enable proper research. Therefore, over recent years a number of structured interviews and rating scales have been developed for use at the various junctures in the encounter with the depressed child and the family: at the time of the original assessment to permit the diagnosis, to measure severity, and to determine outcome. These had their origins in the need for valid and reliable techniques in research, but have found their utility within the clinical setting as well. They facilitate the direct clinical examination of the child, and can be used to collect elements of symptomatology necessary to determine the existence of depression along the various lines of diagnostic criteria. Because of the dictate of rigor demanded by research, a basic requirement of these interviews was that the interviewers routinely ask the same questions of all patients. These instruments include:

- ISC: the Interview Schedule for Children

- ISC − Parent Form

- K-SADS (or Kiddy-SADS): Schedule for Affective Disorders in Schizophrenia, Childhood Version

- DICA: Diagnostic Interview for Children and Adolescents

- DISC-P: the Diagnostic Interview Schedule for Children — Parent Form

- COLPA: Columbia Psychiatric Interview

Some of these interviews are directed at general psychopathology, while others are directed more specifically at depression. These are the Kiddy-SADS, the ISC, and the DICA. Each of these combines uniformity with flexibility (see Petti, 1985).

Rating Scales

A number of rating scales are also used in the area of child depression. Those directed at the children themselves include the Children's Depression Scale (CDS) developed by Lang and Tisher, and the Children's Depression Inventory (CDI), designed by Kovacs and Bach in 1977. Many modifications of the CDI have been made over the years, including the Short Children's Depression Inventory (SCDI).

Scales directed at parents include the Connor's Parent Rating Scale, and Auchenbach's Child Behavior Check List. The Auchenbach in particular has many items referring to depression. These three scales also have versions to be completed by teachers, although only the Auchenbach has a significant number of items relating to depression.

Other scales include the Children's Depression Rating Scale (CDRS), developed by Posnanski et al. (1979); the Children's Affect Rating Scale (CARS), developed by Cytryn and McKnew (1972); and the Bellevue Index of Depression (BID), developed by Petti (1978).

As a general comment, more work remains to be done in all these areas, but the utility and importance in both research and clinical diagnosis of those scales currently available are emphasized.

These diagnostic interviews, rating scales, or self-report inventories, have been reviewed by T. Petti in 1985 in the *Psychopharmacology Bulletin* of the National Institute of Mental Health. They have greatly promoted research into depression of childhood and adolescence.

Further Reading

Anthony, E.J. (1975). Childhood depression. In E.J. Anthony & T. Benedek (Eds.), *Depression and human existence.* Boston: Little Brown.

This chapter, only 46 pages in length, is the most erudite, accurate and readable account of the history of the concept of childhood depression published.

Myers, K.M., Burke, P., & McCauley, E. (1984). Suicidal behavior by hospitalized pre-adolescent children on a psychiatric unit. *Journal of the American Academy of Child Psychiatry, 24,* 474-480.

This brief, well written paper discusses a basic study in the area of depression and suicide.

Psychopharmacology Bulletin, National Institute of Mental Health (1985). Special feature: Rating scales and assessment instruments for use in paediatric psychopharmacology research. 21(4).

For students who wish to have a better review of rating scales of depression.

American Psychiatric Association (1987). *Diagnostic and statistical manual of mental disorders,* 3rd ed., revised (DSM-III-R). Washington, DC: APA Press.

All students should know the details of DSM-III-R, especially the sections dealing with depression.

References

American Psychiatric Association (1987). *Diagnostic and statistical manual of mental disorders,* Third Edition, Revised. Washington, DC: American Psychiatric Association.

Anthony, E.J. (1975). Childhood depression. In E.J. Anthony & T. Benedek (Eds), *Depression and human existence.* Boston: Little, Brown.

Angold, A. (1988). Childhood and adolescent depression: 1. Epidemiological and etiological aspects. *British Journal of Psychiatry, 152,* 601-617.

Bowlby, J. (1969). *Attachment and loss.* Vol. 1: *Attachment.* New York: Basic Books.

Bowlby, J. (1980). *Attachment and loss.* Vol. 3: *Loss, sadness and despression.* New York: Basic Books.

Brent, D. (1987). Correlates of the medical lethality of suicide attempts in children and adolescents. *Journal of the American Academy of Child and Adolescent Psychiatry, 26,* 87-89.

Brent, D.A., Kalas, R., Edelbrock, C., Costella, A.J., Dulcan, M., & Conover, N. (1986). Psychopathology and its relationship to suicidal ideation in childhood and adolescence. *Journal of the American Academy of Child Psychiatry, 55,* 666-673.

Carlson, G.A., & Cantwell, D.P. (1982). Suicidal behavior and depression in children and adolescence. *Journal of the American Academy of Child Psychiatry, 21,* 361-368.

Cohen-Sandler, R., Berman, A.L., & King, R.A. (1982). Life stress and symptomatology: Determinants of suicidal behavior in children. *Journal of the American Academy of Child Psychiatry, 21,* 178-186.

Freedman, R.C., Arnoff, M.S., Clarkin, J.F., Korn, R., & Hurt, S.W. (1983). History of suicidal behavior in depressed borderline inpatients. *American Journal of Psychiatry, 140,* 1023-1024.

Garfinkel, B.D., & Golombek, H. (1974). Suicide and depression in children and adolescence. *Canadian Medical Association Journal, 110,* 1278-1281.

Garfinkel, B.D., & Golombek, H. (1983). Suicidal behavior in adolescents. In B.D. Garfinkel & H. Golombek (Eds.), *The adolescent and mood disorder.* New York: Int. Univ. Press.

Haler, E.A., & Stansfeld, S.A. (1984). Children who poison themselves: 1. A clinical comparison with psychiatric controls; 2. Prediction of attendance for treatment. *British Journal of Psychiatry, 145,* 127-135.

Handford, H.A., Mattison, R., Humphrey, F., & McLaughlin, R. (1986). Depressive syndrome in children entering a residential school subsequent parent death, divorce, or separation. *Journal of the American Academy of Child Psychiatry, 25,* 409-414.

Hoberman, H.M. & Garfinkel, B.D. (1988). Completed suicide in youth. *Canadian Journal of Psychiatry.,* 33, 494-504.

Kashani, K., & Carlson, G.A. (1987). Seriously depressed preschoolers. *American Journal of Psychiatry, 143,* 348-358.

Kovacs, M., Feinberg, T.L., Crouse-Novak, N.A., Paulauskas, S.L., Pollock, M., & Finkelstein, R. (1984a). A longitudinal study of the risk for a subsequent major depression. *Archives of General Psychiatry, 41,* 229-237.

Kovacs, M., Feinberg, T.L., Crouse-Novak, N.A., Paulauskas, S.L., & Finkelstein, R. (1984b). Depressive disorders in childhood. *Archives of General Psychiatry, 41,* 643-649.

Marriage, K., Fine, S., Moretti, M., & Haley, G. (1986). Relationship between depression and conduct disorder in children and adolescents. *Journal of the American Academy of Child Psychiatry, 25,* 687-691.

Mattsson, A., Seese, L.R., & Hawkins, J.W. (1969). Suicidal behavior as a child psychiatric emergency. *Archives of General Psychiatry, 20,* 100-109.

Myers, K.M., Burke P., & McCauley, E. (1984). Suicidal behavior by hospitalized pre-adolescent children on a psychiatric unit. *Journal of the American Academy of Child Psychiatry, 24,* 474-480.

Otto, U. (1972). Suicidal acts by children and adolescents. *Acta Psychiatrica Scandinavia, Supplement 233.*

Petti, T. (1985). Scales of potential use in the pharmacological treatment of depressed children and adolescents. *Psychopharmacology Bulletin, National Institute of Mental Health, 21,* 951-955.

Pfeffer, C.R. (1980). Parental suicide: An organizing event in the development of latency-age children. *Suicide and Life-Threatening Behavior, 11,* 43-50.

Pfeffer, C.R., Conte, H.R., & Plutchik, R. (1979). Suicidal behavior in latency-age children: An empirical study. *Journal of the American Academy of Child Psychiatry, 18,* 679-692.

Pfeffer, C.R., & Jerrett, I. (1980). Suicidal behavior in latency-age children: An outpatient population. *Journal of the American Academy of Child Psychiatry, 19,* 703-710.

Pfeffer, C.R. (1981). Suicidal behavior of children: A review with implications for research and practice. *American Journal of Psychiatry,* 138, 154-159.

Pfeffer, C.R., Solomon, G., Plutchik, R., Mizruchi, M.S., & Weiner, A. (1982). Suicidal behavior in latency-age psychiatric inpatients: A replication and cross-validation. *Journal of the American Academy of Child Psychiatry, 21, 564-569.*

Pfeffer, C.R., Zukerman, S., Plutchik, R., & Mizruchi, M.S. (1984). Suicidal behavior in normal school children: A comparison with child psychiatric inpatients. *Journal of the American Academy of Child Psychiatry, 23,* 416-423.

Poznanski, E., Grossman, J., Bucksbaum, Y., Banegas, M., Freeman, L., & Gibbons, R. (1984). Preliminary studies of the reliability and validity of the Children's Depression Rating Scale. *Journal of the American Academy of Child Psychiatry, 23,* 191-197.

Psychopharmacology Bulletin, National Institute of Mental Health (1985). Special feature: *Rating scales and assessment instruments for use in paediatric psychopharmacology research, 21, 4.*

Rie, H. (1966). Depression in childhood: A survey of some pertinent contributions. *Journal of the American Academy of Child Psychiatry, 5,* 653-685.

Robbins, D.R., & Alessi, N.E. (1985). Depressive symptoms and suicidal behavior in adolescence. *American Journal of Psychiatry, 142,* 588-592.

Shaffer, D. (1974). Suicide in children and early adolescence. *Journal of Child Psychology and Psychiatry, 15,* 275-291.

Shaffer, D., Garland, A., Gould, M., Fisher, P., & Trautman, P. (1988). Preventing teenage suicide: A critical review.

Journal of the American Academy of Child and Adolescent Psychiatry, 27, 675-687.

Shaffer, D. (1974). Suicide in childhood and early adolescence. *Journal of Child Psychology and Psychiatry, 291,* 15-75.

Shaffi, N., Carrigan, S., Whittinghill, J.R., & Derrick, A. (1985). Psychological autopsy of completed suicide in children and adolescents. *American Journal of Psychiatry, 142,* 1061-1064.

Spitz, R. (1945). Hospitalism: An inquiry into the genesis of psychiatric conditions in early childhood. Psychoanalytic Study of the Child, 1, 53-75

Spitz, R. (1946). Anaclitic depression: An inquiry into the genesis of psychiatric conditions in early childhood. II. *Psychoanalytic Study of the Child, 2,* 313-342.

Spitzer, R.L., Endicott, J., & Robbins, E. (1978). Research diagnostic criteria: Rationale of reliability. *Archives of General Psychiatry, 35,* 773-782.

Triolo-Santo, J., McKenry, P.C., Tishler, C.L., & Blyth, D.A. (1984). Social and psychological determinants of adolescent suicide: Age and sex differences. *Journal of Early Adolescence.*

Valez, C.N. and Cohen, P.(1988). Suicidal behavior and ideation in a community sample of children: Maternal and youth reports. *Journal of the American Academy of Child and Adolescent Psychiatry, 27,* 349-356.

Weinberg, W.A., Rutman J., Sullivan, L., Penick, E.C., & Dietz, S.G. (1973). Depression in children referred to an education diagnostic centre. *Journal of Pediatrics, 83,* 1065-1172.

Welner, A., Welner, Z., & Fishman, R. (1979). Psychiatric adolescent inpatients: Eight to ten year follow-up. *Archives of General Psychiatry, 36,* 698-700.

Chapter 4

Manifestation of Risk Factors

Cynthia R. Pfeffer, M.D.

Many studies have appeared in recent years to elucidate the factors associated with fatal and nonfatal suicidal behavior in youth—e.g., symptoms, behaviors, diagnoses, environmental stresses, family background, and constitutional variables. These epidemiologically oriented reports are concerned with trends in groups and, as described in the first chapter, are invaluable in understanding the processes associated with risk.

The epidemiological approach involves an orientation different from that utilized in clinical work. A given youngster's symptomatology, behaviors, degree of psychopathology, and life experience may of course be quite distinct from the group trends specified in epidemiological studies. However, the art and science of appraising a particular patient for suicidal risk necessitates that one evaluate individual variance and make effective clinical judgments, and to do this it is necessary to evaluate the relative contributions of factors that may provoke suicidal ideation and/or action. Knowledge from epidemiological studies is essential as a basis and guide for the clinician to make inferences, reach conclusions, and plan intervention strategies.

It is necessary for instance to delineate those risk factors associated with specified periods along the life cycle: that is, to identify whether a given factor is prevalent in a group at a certain stage of development. For example, can depression exist in preadolescent children? Another need is to identify whether and to what degree a given factor is associated with suicidal risk. A third issue is whether the *manifestations* of risk factors differ in different developmental periods; a fascinating issue for which relatively few systematic data currently exist. For example, one question that requires more sophisticated research methodology is whether the expression of suicidal behavior is the same across children, adolescents, and adults. Studies utilizing cross-sectional and longitudinal designs address different facets of this issue, evaluating psychopathology either in populations of youngsters who are in different stages of development, or for a given group as it matures. Developmental variations should be known and understood by the clinician.

With the above issues in mind, this chapter will describe several important risk factors for youth suicidal behavior that have been identified in epidemiological studies. Specifically, it will discuss how such factors may be expressed differentially in children and in adolescents, and whenever possible comparisons for these two developmental periods will be emphasized. It is hoped that clinicians may usefully integrate such information with the unique data gathered about a given patient at risk.

The Spectrum of Suicidal Behavior

Not only may the risk factors associated with suicidal behavior differ depending on the characteristics of a group, but the *features* of the behavior may differ. For example, it is known from national data that rates of completed suicide are higher for the 15- to 24-year-old age group than for 5- to 14-year-olds. This difference in prevalence may affect a clinician's level of concern about risk for patients of different ages. Thus, a teenager who talks about wishing to kill him/ herself may arouse a higher level of concern than a similar report from a preadolescent. However, the fallacy of this logic lies with two issues. First, suicidal behavior in general is a relatively rare event, so that the ability to predict it over a long time is not possible. Second, as noted before, although epidemiological data may suggest that suicide for a developmental group as a whole has a specific rate, because of individual variation a particular patient may not conform to these trends. It is thus essential to consider *any* youngster who expresses suicidal intent, ideation, or action to be at risk. The patient should be carefully evaluated and risk factors diminished as rapidly as possible.

Included under the rubric of suicidal behavior may be both ideation of self-destruction, and actual acts. There has been much debate about whether ideation, attempts, and completed suicide occur within a continuous gradient or are distinct entities. Pfeffer and associates (1979, 1982 1986a) argue that childhood suicidal behavior can be defined as ranging along a spectrum, from suicidal ideation, to suicidal threats, to suicidal attempts, to suicide. Their studies, based on direct interviews of preadolescents and their parents, focused on nonfatal suicidal behavior. Several behavioral and symptomatic correlates were identified, such as depression, death preoccupations, and poor impulse control, which increased in severity in direct relation to the intensification of severity of suicidal behavior — thus providing strong support for the idea of a continuous spectrum. These findings were noted across samples of psychiatric inpatients, outpatients, and nonpatients.

Validation of these results was obtained from corroborating studies. For example, Brent and colleagues (1986), with a sample of 231 children referred for outpatient psychiatric treatment, interviewed each patient and a parent using the Diagnostic Interview Schedule for Children (see Chapter 3). Symptom scores were evaluated for suicidal ideation and acts, depression, conduct problems, attentional difficulties, and substance abuse, and a hierarchical scale for suicidal ideation and acts was constructed that ranged from suicidal ideation to threats to attempts. Youngsters who responded affirmatively to questions of greater severity were likely to respond positively to questions of less severity. In an evaluation of the relationship between ratings of suicidal ideation and acts to other psychiatric symptoms, the severity of suicidal tendencies was found to be directly associated with levels of severity of such symptoms as depression, conduct problems, alcohol abuse, overanxious disorder, major depressive disorder, and dysthymic disorder. In summary, this study supported the view that youth suicidal tendencies can be considered along a continuum.

Another major issue that requires clarification is whether youths who only attempt suicide have similar characteristics to those who actually carry it out. This issue has many implications for both research and clinical practice: it may enhance our understanding of risk factors, helping to identify those at highest risk, and thereby give clinicians better direction in their evaluations. Recent work by Brent and associates (1988) found *some* similar characteristics associated with both adolescent suicide attempters and victims. Twenty-seven victims evaluated by psychological autopsy methods were compared to 56 psychiatric in-patients who had either seriously considered or seriously attempted suicide, and had been systematically interviewed during their hospitalization. Similarities in the two groups were found for a variety of factors, including high rates of affective disorders (including family histories of affective disorders), antisocial behavior, and suicide. However, differences were also noted: the victims had shown a higher prevalence of bipolar disorder and affective disorder with co-occurring disorders, utilized mental health treatment less frequently, and firearms were more often reported by relatives to be in the home. This study, therefore, suggests that while completed suicide in youth has similar characteristics to nonfatal attempts, the differences in particular features should be highlighted as a means of identifying those most at risk. These discriminating factors are ones that clinicians should be particularly concerned with in identifying means of intervention and prevention.

The importance of the concept of a continuous spectrum of suicidal behavior is that a clinician may be able to estimate the degree of seriousness of risk by evaluating the intensity or severity in the manifestation of those factors known to correlate with suicidal ideation and acts. For example, as the intensity of depression escalates it may be expected that the seriousness of suicidal behavior will increase proportionally. One can therefore hope that by intervening to decrease a risk factor, the seriousness of suicidal behavior will diminish. Additional studies of biological correlates and other psychosocial features are needed to substantiate these recent research findings.

Another manifestation of youth suicidal behavior is that suicidal ideation and acts can be depicted within the framework of an *episode* (Pfeffer, 1986a). A suicidal episode can be defined as a discrete event or period that has an onset, a time period or duration of expression, and an offset time. This concept of a discrete entity enables a clinician to focus on the episode, to evaluate its course, and to identify when it is over. It also enables monitoring of the effects of diminishing risk factors on the intensity, duration, and outcome of suicidal tendencies. A youngster may manifest a single suicidal episode or multiple ones, and within a single episode can have multiple suicidal ideas and/or acts. The complexities of defining a suicidal episode require more investigation; for example, it is not known how long a period of time should elapse in which there is no evidence of self-destructive tendencies before the onset of another episode can be defined. (An analogy can be made with psychiatric disorders, where a period of several months that are relatively symptom-free must occur before one can be sure that an episode is over.) The "chronic" suicidal youngster is defined as one who exhibits numerous individual episodes over an extended time period, rather than experiencing a single long episode. This phenomenon is almost invariably associated with risk factors that are chronically present and potentiate the episode, such as affect instability or impulsivity.

The *method* used in a suicidal act is another important element in describing an episode. Recent analyses of national data relating adolescent suicide to the techniques used show that the most frequent method is firearms (Boyd & Moscicki, 1986; Brent et al., 1987). Furthermore, of all techniques, firearms have increased in prevalence in direct relation to the increased rate of suicide among adolescents and young adults. In fact, as described in a detailed psychological autopsy study (Brent et al., 1987), a frequent characteristic of teenage suicide is availability of firearms and their use while the victim is intoxicated with alcohol or other substances. In this study, coroner's records of 159 youth suicides (aged 15-19 years at the time of death) occurring over a 24-year period were reviewed. Firearm use was the most commonly used method, involving 55.4% of all of the deaths from 1978 to 1983. In addition, the increase in suicide rates over the entire period of the study was paralleled by an increase in alcohol found in blood assays of the victims. The study noted that the victims with high blood alcohol levels were more likely to have used firearms as the method of suicide than those without high blood alcohol levels. This highlights the clinical need to evaluate and treat substance abuse, and to identify whether a youngster is in proximity to handguns, rifles, and other such weapons. Inhibiting easy access to firearms may enhance elements of suicide prevention.

Other methods utilized by adolescents to carry out suicidal acts include ingestion of potentially toxic substances, hanging, stabbing oneself with knives or other sharp objects, and jumping from high places such as roofs, windows, bridges, or cliffs (Pfeffer et al., 1988; Shaffer, 1988). These methods are also commonly used by preadolescents (Pfeffer, 1986), although the use of firearms is less common among young children. This may account for why preadolescent suicide is so much less prevalent than among teenagers and young adults.

A key descriptor of a suicidal episode is that it involves *intent* to carry out a self-destructive act that may lead to death or serious self-harm. However, it is often difficult to elicit self-destructive intent, especially in preadolescents, and teenagers commonly deny such intent even after the idea or act has been exhibited. Denial of intentionality is especially common as more time passes since the acute event. Assessment of intentionality is necessary, and even if it appears absent a clinician should not automatically reject the existence of a suicidal episode. It is clinically wiser to suspect suicidal tendencies so that intervention may be offered, rather than minimize the potential risks and miss out on necessary treatment.

Another consideration in describing a suicidal episode is its *lethality:* that is, the capability of the self-inflicted action of causing serious harm or death. Of great importance in appraising suicidal lethality in children and adolescents is to consider both the realistic or objective degree of harm that can ensue, and the concurrent subjective opinion of lethality by the suicidal individual him/herself. Jumping out of a sixth-floor window would cause serious harm or death and would objectively be considered highly lethal: however, a child may not be aware of the danger of enacting such a method. Conversely, if a child believes that taking one Aspirin tablet is very dangerous, the clinician may consider such behavior to have moderately high lethality as the child *intended* to enact something self-destructive. Thus, the ability to perceive cause and effect is a significant issue.

The issue of developmental stage has other implications as well. An important question that is often asked is whether it is required that the individual be able to conceptualize death as final in order for the act to be defined as suicidal. Studies of community populations (Koocher, 1973) suggest that concepts of the finality of death are not well established until at least the age of nine, and even some older children and adolescents do not have a consistent concept of its finality. However, the intent to carry out self-harm does not have to be congruent with a mature concept of death. The concept of death may vary and a child may not know the actual consequences of self-destructive behavior, but what appears to be essential in defining ideation and/or behavior as suicidal is that the youngster have an intent to die or to cause self-injury. Death is the goal, whatever dying may mean to that child.

Finally, the circumstances in which an act is planned or enacted also characterizes how a suicidal episode is manifested. For example, did the youngster carefully plan the self-destructive behavior, or was the act impulsive? Did the idea of carrying it out occur after a stressful interaction with someone? Was the intention to frighten or take revenge on somebody? Was it an act of ultimate desperation? Was it planned or carried out in close proximity to someone else who might have been able to abort it? The possibility that someone may have been available as a rescuer indicates a decreased potential for self-damage.

In summary, suicidal episodes have many facets that affect how they are manifested. Important factors include duration, method of enactment, degree of lethality, intent for self-harm, potential to abort the act, and motive. All these issues must be carefully evaluated by the clinician.

Classes of Risk Factors

A useful approach to evaluating suicidal risk is to conceptualize risk factors as belonging to groups that can be defined by some common basis. Furthermore, these groups (or "clusters") may modify and/or potentiate other clusters, so the presence of one or several clusters enhances the likelihood that a suicidal episode may occur. Based on her empirical data, Pfeffer (1986) proposed one model that identified an *affect* group, a *coping mechanism* group, an *interpersonal* group, and a *developmental* group, and suggested that they interact to create a dynamic equilibrium in which the relative influence of a particular cluster may vary at a particular time. An example of this would be a teenager who is exhibiting symptoms of a major depressive disorder (affect group) and also experiencing intense stress with his or her family (interpersonal group). The impact of these two groups of risk factors may create a high likelihood for suicidal ideation or acts. However, if the interpersonal problems are alleviated, the youngster's degree of depression may also diminish and the suicidal risk be lessened.

With these concerns in mind, an issue that has received some research attention is the *relative risk* contributed by each of these clusters. In one important study, Shaffer (1988) reported how risk factors for male and female suicide victims differ. Utilizing the psychological autopsy method, he and his colleagues identified characteristics of adolescents who

had killed themselves. They found that certain factors promoted suicide with particular degrees of relative risk, reported
here as the rate of suicide per 100,000 population that would
occur if a particular risk factor were present. His data reflected
the following relative risks: for males, history of a prior
suicide attempt—270; major depressive disorder—100;
substance abuse—70; antisocial behavior—40; and family
history of suicide—35. For females, the relative risks were
major depressive disorder—80; history of a past suicide
attempt—20; antisocial behavior—8; family history of
suicide—6; and substance abuse—3. Similar studies looking
at other aspects would be helpful: for instance, describing
the relative risk for factors associated with suicide *attempts*
in youth, or, as with gender, comparing relative risks in
various populations with defined characteristics (such as
adolescent psychiatric inpatients compared to teenagers in the
general population). Such efforts to identify relative risk in
specified populations would put into perspective the types
of factors deserving of extensive intervention, and may offer
a useful approach for suicide prevention.

Another important facet is *how* risk factors are expressed.
Manifestations may differ with respect to characteristics of
a given population of youngsters, both in prevalence and in
signs and symptoms. An important issue requiring additional
inquiry is the variation with regard to age. Utilizing a
developmental perspective, the remaining part of this chapter
will discuss how suicidal risk factors manifest themselves in
children and adolescents in general, and will identify whether
these factors differ with respect to differing developmental
periods. For purposes of illustration, only one or two risk
factors within each type of group will be described.

Depression

With the advent of DSM-III, classification of psychiatric disorders achieved a detailed degree of standardization, which in turn was used in developing research instruments able to reliably evaluate child and adolescent psychopathology in a comparative way. These advancements helped dispel the old belief that children are developmentally incapable of exhibiting depression. Numerous studies (e.g., Pfeffer, 1986) suggest that depressive disorders exist in both children and adolescents, and that their phenomenology, natural course, physiology, family history, and treatment are similar to those seen in adults. In addition, empirical data have highlighted the occurrence of suicidal ideation and acts in youth, and suggested that they are are associated with depressive symptoms and affective disorders (Pfeffer, 1986).

An important concern is to identify *which* particular features of depression are associated with youth suicidal behavior. It must be appreciated that depression can be conceptualized either as a *symptom* of depressed mood and/or appearance, as a *syndrome* consisting of several symptoms associated with depressed mood, or as a *disorder* that involves depressed mood and a certain number of specified associated symptoms (Carlson & Cantwell, 1980). Therefore, the manifestations of depression may vary depending upon the level of classification utilized.

Depressed mood and the appearance of sadness, tearfulness, and being "blue" are features associated with almost all suicidal children and adolescents. This observation has been documented in various populations: clinical and non-clinical, juvenile offenders, and suicide victims (Pfeffer, 1986).

Other affective disorders such as major depressive and bipolar disorders have also been found to be associated with suicidal ideation and acts (Pfeffer, 1986). An important finding from one follow-up study of adolescent psychiatric inpatients (Welner, Welner, & Fishman, 1979) illustrated the high degree of suicidal lethality associated with affective disorders. In that study, 25% of 12 patients with bipolar disorder committed suicide within 8-10 years after hospital discharge—a higher rate than for patients in the same hospital unit who were diagnosed with schizophrenia, conduct disorder, and a variety of other psychiatric disorders including major depression.

Robbins and Alessi (1985) evaluated the specific types of symptoms involved in a diagnosis of major depressive disorder that were associated with suicidal ideation and/or attempts among adolescent psychiatric inpatients. Among 64 patients, approximately half had made suicide attempts and 47% had a major depressive disorder. Assessment of suicidal behavior and of psychiatric symptoms and disorders in this study utilized semi-structured interview techniques with the SADS (Spitzer & Endicott, 1977). The results indicated that in general, suicidal ideas were most associated with the specific symptoms of depressive disorder: depressed mood, negative self-image, hopelessness, insomnia, poor concentration, anhedonia, guilt, low energy, poor appetite, social withdrawal, and alcohol abuse. Suicidal attempts were associated with depressed mood, alcohol abuse, negative self-evaluation, and drug abuse. Additional investigation is warranted; for example, no data have yet been reported using a similar research design for preadolescents, or for youth suicide victims. Early identification of suicidal risk may be well served by a clinician's ability to recognize the manifestations of depressive symptomatology most associated with suicidal behavior.

Conduct disorders such as truancy, gang membership, lying, stealing, and violence have been associated with suicidal behavior in adolescence (Pfeffer, 1986), but are not as clearly apparent in children. Substance abuse is also an important risk factor and may, in fact, be a very prominent aspect of characterizing youth who kill themselves.

Evidence of developmental differences in the relation between suicidal behavior and affective and antisocial/substance-abuse symptoms has been presented. The San Diego Suicide Study (Rich, Young, & Fowler, 1986) utilized psychological autopsy techniques to compare 133 suicide victims under 30 years of age and 150 over the age of 30. The findings indicated that there was more drug abuse and antisocial tendencies among the younger victims, while the older ones had a higher prevalence of affective disorders and organic problems. Such data are essential in identifying approaches that can be specified for intervention and prevention programs for youth with varying developmental and clinical features.

In summary, affects such as depression and aggression are significantly associated with youth suicidal behavior, but additional research is warranted to evaluate the specific characteristics of these factors. The data also suggest that developmental factors are important in variation in levels of risk and in the types of risk factors.

Adaptive Mechanisms

Psychological mechanisms that integrate one's personal experiences with efforts to adapt to circumstances are important life-sustaining functions. These include cognitive faculties, perceptions, conceptualization of experiences to form judgments that determine action, and the ability to respond with consistency and planning. A number of such adaptive mechanisms have been found to be associated with suicidal behavior. Two features will be highlighted here, since they represent basic issues. One involves cognitive perception of experiences, such as whether an individual perceives events as positive and hopeful. These perceptions are important factors in sustaining life and enhancing the quality of one's circumstances. The other feature involves one's responses to circumstances; specifically, how one appraises, plans, and behaves in circumstances with the goal of promoting one's interests positively and beneficially. The two features invariably are related, and affect the behavioral patterns and course of life experiences.

The antitheses of these factors are pessimism, hopelessness, and impulsivity. Each of these has been been found to be associated with lethal suicidal behavior in adults: additional research is required with suicidal children and adolescents. Beck described aspects of hopelessness and focused on its components of pessimistic view of the future, self-depreciation, and negative perceptions of one's current experiences. Based on these ideas, Beck and associates (1974) created a scale to rate the degree of pessimism an individual feels. Utilizing this research instrument, studies have identified the important predictive features of hopelessness for suicidal behavior. For example, a study of 154 psychiatric inpatients who were either suicidal or nonsuicidal (Wetzel, 1976), suggested that the severity of depression was associated with suicidal attempts, and that hopelessness was highly correlated with suicidal behavior. Of note was that hopelessness correlated higher with suicidal intent or behavior than did depression. This study suggested the important interactions between hopelessness and depression as risk factors for suicidal behavior. The strong predictive aspect of hopelessness was suggested by a 10-year prospective follow-up of suicidal patients (Beck et al., 1985): in this study, approximately 6.9% of 107 patients had killed themselves by the time of follow-up, with hopelessness being the only factor that distinguished them from the 16.4% of patients who died from other causes. These studies suggest that hopelessness is an important risk factor for suicidal behavior in adults, and requires careful assessment.

Considering the developmental influences on young people, the role of hopelessness for suicidal ideation and acts has been found to have varying degrees of risk enhancement. Kazdin and associates (1983) developed a version of the Beck Hopelessness Scale to be used for children and adolescents. Utilizing this instrument with 66 preadolescent psychiatric inpatients, hopelessness was found to be more significantly associated with suicidal behavior than was depression, results that are similar to those found in adults.

Contrasting results to those found in studies of adult and preadolescent suicidal individuals have been found for adolescents. In the only reported study (Rotheram-Borus & Trautman, 1988) of the relation between hopelessness and adolescent suicidal behavior, 44 female outpatient suicide attempters reported high levels of hopelessness and depression, but neither predicted risk for suicidal behavior.

These studies suggest that the manifestations of hopelessness as a risk factor for youth suicidal behavior may differ with regard to types of populations and/or developmental stages. Nevertheless, it seems apparent that a pessimistic view of one's life is an important issue for those considering to end their lives.

Impulsivity as a distinct entity has been insufficiently studied with regard to youth suicidal behavior. Pfeffer and associates (1986) derived a rating of impulse control by assessing such aspects as ability to delay action, make decisions, endure frustration, and the degree to which one retreats into fantasy. The results of studies of preadolescent patients and nonpatients suggest that poor impulse control is associated with suicidal risk. Systematic studies of adolescents are needed to more specifically appraise this factor.

From a clinical perspective, impulsivity is an important element of nonpredictability, as impulsive tendencies make it difficult for a clinician to feel confident that a youngster's ability to avoid suicidal action is consistent. An issue that needs further clarification is whether impulsive individuals are at greater risk for fatal suicidal acts than those who carefully plan their self-destructive behavior. It is known that a large percentage of nonfatal attempts are carried out impulsively and with poor planning; thus, perhaps planning is the essential ingredient leading to suicide, and acts that are hastily conceptualized are not fatal. However, the degree of lethality associated with impulsive suicidal acts requires additional study.

In summary, factors of cognition and behavior such as hopelessness and impulsivity are associated with suicidal ideation and acts in children and adolescents and have general effects on a youngster's adaptive skills with regard to judgment and planning behavior. Vulnerability in managing stressful circumstances arises when pessimism and/or impulsivity are evident.

Interpersonal Factors

Suicidal behavior in young people is often precipitated by a variety of immediate stresses that are perceived in crisis proportions. Many of these events are not unusual in the lives of normal youngsters, such as arguments with parents, punishment, disappointments, rejections, and losses, so the actual mechanisms that create higher risk for suicidal behavior require extensive study. One possibility is that youngsters who experience these interpersonal factors have been highly sensitized to them because of chronic stressful occurrences. It may also be that suicidal-prone youngsters have other concurrent risk factors (such as depressive disorders) that potentiate the effects of stress from these events.

Therefore, interpersonal problems should be considered important potentiating factors for suicidal risk, and should be systematically discussed and evaluated. The types of precipitants that are associated with suicidal risk may differ with respect to developmental stages. Preadolescents, for example, are highly dependent on their parents and are just beginning to gradually separate from the home environment, so interpersonal factors involving parents, siblings, teachers, and friends are important areas in a young child's life. For adolescents, while these relationships are also very important, the degree of dependency on home and other family environmental relations is different, and they are highly influenced by out-of-home relationships. Problems with boyfriends/girlfriends should be specifically discussed, and assistance in coping with these difficulties offered. Other aspects of peer relationships are also important in creating tensions that may precipitate suicidal behavior, such as being exposed (directly or indirectly) to the suicidal tendencies of a friend or acquaintance. Some reports (Shaffii et al., 1985) suggest that such exposure raises risk, and assessment of this may help an adolescent discuss worries about him/herself with regard to self-destructive behavior. It may elucidate feelings of self-doubt, animosities, loneliness, and disillusionment.

Another important aspect of personal relations is maintenance of self-esteem. Probably one of the most critical factors in precipitating suicidal ideation arising from interpersonal problems is humiliation—feelings of disgrace and public disparagement may shatter a youngster's healthy sense of narcissism and sense of identity, and loss of a basic sense of one's worthwhileness is a powerful force to increase thoughts of self-annihiliation. Stabilizing factors that may be helpful in preventing suicidal behavior, therefore, involve establishing supportive social interactions. A clinician is essential in providing this, as well as in coordinating the network of others who can establish stable supports. Praise, assistance in solving problems, mediation in interpersonal disputes, and extensive modification of the youngster's environment are all helpful in re-establishing life preserving efforts.

Developmental Experiences

A variety of influences during the course of a lifetime may affect vulnerability to suicidal behavior. The clinician working with a patient at risk should identify past experiences that may have affected the youngster's development and thereby enhance suicidal vulnerability.

Recent evidence (Klerman, 1988) suggests that recently born cohorts of youngsters may be more vulnerable to depression and suicide as they enter adolescence. Implications of this are that something occurring early in the lives of these youngsters enhances vulnerability. The elements involved in this, however, are not known.

Another example that illustrates early influences as predictors of adolescent suicide was derived from the study by Salk and associates (1985), who compared the neonatal records of 52 adolescents who had committed suicide to those of of two matched control groups. Respiratory distress for more than one hour after birth, no prenatal care before 20 weeks of pregnancy, and chronic illness of the mother during pregnancy were found to be significantly associated with adolescent suicide. The impact of variables early in life requires attention clinically as well as research investigation, as further under-standing of these effects may be very helpful in preventing problems later on. For example, an implication suggested by this study is that early factors may affect physiological mechanisms that bear upon risk for suicidal behavior years later. Another possibility is that the poor medical condition of the mother before and during the pregnancy may be a reflection of social behaviors that continue to be a problem throughout the life of the child. This study implies that perhaps the interactions between social factors and physiological features should be acknowledged as hallmarks for suicidal risk.

Increasing alarm has focused on the serious problems in parenting highlighted by child abuse. Current evidence (Pfeffer, 1986; Pfeffer et al., 1988) indicates that physical and sexual abuse are associated with youth suicidal behavior, so a history of abuse should alert a clinician to the possibility that a youngster may be vulnerable. Such a history may have longstanding effects: severe punishment or physical acts by an adult has effects psychologically on the child's self-esteem, may create an identification with the abuser, and can interfere with the child's organization of fantasy life. In addition, physiological sequelae to physical abuse may affect a youngster's capacity to maintain impulse control, judgment, and affect stability. The actual mechanisms of the effects of abuse require extensive study.

In summary, experiential processes have additive and modifying influences on suicidal risk, and children with histories of severe psychosocial trauma early in life should be considered to be at high risk for suicidal behavior.

Conclusion

The clinical and research efforts in recent years to clarify factors associated with child and adolescent suicidal risk have provided clinicians and others with insights sufficient to adequately evaluate suicidal youngsters. However, there is a need to collect data about relative influences of these risk factors. This chapter has focused on pointing out that risk factors may express themselves with varied prevalence rates and characteristics in different youth populations.

The developmental continuities and discontinuities in risk factors must be appreciated in order to effectively evaluate and plan interventions and suicide prevention programs. The fact that males commit suicide more frequently than females suggests an underlying discontinuity in social and biological risk; the fact that females *attempt* it more often has been an oft repeated statement which, in fact, requires specification about which population of females one means. Evidence suggests that the ratio of male to female adolescent psychiatric inpatients who are hospitalized for suicide attempts do not differ significantly. Depression has been associated with suicidal behavior in individuals of all ages; however, substance abuse appears to be more characteristic of younger victims. Thus, assessment and interventions must ensue from a systematic appraisal of the qualitative and quantitative manifestations of suicide risk factors evident in different types of populations.

Recommended Reading

Boyd, J.H., & Moscicki, E.K. (1986). Firearms and youth suicide. *American Journal of Public Health, 76*, 1240-1242.

This epidemiological analysis of National Vital Statistics data evaluates relationships between youth suicide rates and the use of suicidal methods over time. The results suggest that there is a direct relation between these rates and the use of firearms as the most prevalent method.

Brent, D.A., Kalas, R., Edelbrock, C., Costello, A., Dulcan, M.K., & Conover, N. (1986). Psychopathology and its relationship to suicidal ideation in childhood and adolescence. *Journal of the American Academy of Child Psychiatry, 25*, 666-673.

An evaluation of the relationship between suicidal ideation and acts and psychiatric symptoms in child psychiatric patients, which found that suicidal tendencies increased in severity as a continuous function and were related to the severity of psychiatric symptoms.

Pfeffer, C.R., Newcorn, J., Kaplan, G., Mizruchi, M.S., & Plutchik, R. (1988). Suicidal behavior in adolescent psychiatric inpatients. *Journal of the American Academy of Child and Adolescent Psychiatry, 27,* 357-361.

Epidemiological data of consecutively admitted adolescent psychiatric inpatients, looking at suicidal behavior and associated factors. Some differences were noted for girls and boys in the levels of aggression and depression.

Pfeffer C.R., Plutchik R., Mizruchi M.S., and Lipkins R. (1986): Suicidal behavior in child psychiatric inpatients and outpatients and in nonpatients. *American Journal of Psychiatry, 143,* 733-738.

A comparison of the prevalence of suicidal behavior in child psychiatric outpatients, inpatients, and nonpatients. Significant differences were found in prevalence, but similar risk factors were found for all three groups.

Rich, C.L., Young, D., & Fowler, R.C. (1986). San Diego Suicide Study: I. Young versus old subjects. *Archives of General Psychiatry, 43,* 577-582.

This interesting study used psychological autopsy methods to compare suicide victims younger and older than 30 years. Significant differences were noted: younger victims used alcohol more and had a greater prevalence of antisocial behavior than the older victims.

Shaffii, M., Carrigan, S., Whittingbill, J.R.,& Derrick, A. (1985). Psychological autopsy of completed suicide in children and adolescents. *American Journal of Psychiatry, 142,* 1061-1064.

A good study to read in its entirety. The psychological autopsy method was used to compare adolescent suicide victims with non-suicidal adolescents. The former had a greater history of suicidal tendencies and also experienced a greater prevalence of family disturbances.

References

Beck, A.T., Steer, R.A., Kovacs, M., & Garrison, B. (1985). Hopelessness and eventual suicide: A 10-year prospective study of patients hospitalized with suicidal ideation. *American Journal of Psychiatry, 142,* 559-563.

Beck, A.T., Weissman, A., Lester, D., & Trexler, L. (1974). The measurement of pessimism: The hopelessness scale. *Journal of Consulting and Clinical Psychology, 42,* 861-865.

Boyd, J.H., & Moscicki, E.K. (1986). Firearms and youth suicide. *American Journal of Public Health, 76,* 1240-1242.

Brent, D.A., Kalas, R., Edelbrock, C., Costello, A., Dulcan, M.K., & Conover, N. (1986). Psychopathology and its relationship to suicidal ideation in childhood and adolescence. *Journal of the American Academy of Child Psychiatry, 25,* 666-673.

Brent, D.A., Perper, J.A., & Allman, C.J. (1987). Alcohol, firearms, and suicide among youth: Temporal trends in Allegheny County, Pennsylvania, 1960 to 1983. *Archives of General Psychiatry, 257,* 3369-3372.

Brent, D.A., Perper, J.A., Goldstein, C.E., Kolko, D.J., Allan, M.J., Allman, C.J., & Zelenak, J.P. (1988). Risk factors for adolescent suicide: A comparison of adolescent victims with suicidal inpatients. *Archives of General Psychiatry, 45,* 581-588.

Carlson, G.A., & Cantwell, D.P. (1980). A survey of depressive symptoms, syndrome, and disorder in a child psychiatric population. *Journal of Child Psychology and Psychiatry, 21,* 19-25.

Kazdin, A.E., French, N.H., Unis, A.S., Esveldt-Dawson, K., & Sherick, R.B. (1983). Hopelessness, depression, and suicidal intent among psychiatrically disturbed inpatient children. *Journal of Consulting and Clinical Psychology, 51,* 504-510.

Klerman, G.L. (1988). The current age of youthful melancholia: Evidence for increase in depression among adolescents and young adults. *British Journal of Psychiatry, 152,* 4-14.

Koocher, G.P. (1973). Childhood, death, and cognitive development. *Developmental Psychology, 9,* 369-375.

Pfeffer, C.R. (1986a). *The suicidal child.* New York, NY: Guilford Press.

Pfeffer, C.R., Conte, H.R., Plutchik R., & Jerrett, I. (1979). Suicidal behavior in latency-age children: An empirical study. *Journal of the American Academy of Child Psychiatry, 18,* 679-692.

Pfeffer, C.R., Conte, H.R., Plutchik, R., & Jerrett I. (1986). Suicidal behavior in latency-age children: An empirical study: An outpatient population. *Journal of the American Academy of Child Psychiatry, 19,* 703-710.

Pfeffer, C.R., Newcorn, J., Kaplan, G., Mizruchi, M.S., & Plutchik, R. (1988). Suicidal behavior in adolescent psychiatric inpatients. *Journal of the American Academy of Child and Adolescent Psychiatry, 27,* 357-361.

Pfeffer, C.R., Plutchik, R., Mizruchi, M.S., & Lipkins, R. (1986b). Suicidal behavior in child psychiatric inpatients and outpatients and in nonpatients. *American Journal of Psychiatry, 143,* 733-738.

Pfeffer, C.R., Solomon, G., Plutchik, R., Mizruchi, M.S., & Weiner, A. (1982). Suicidal behavior in latency-age psychiatric inpatients: A replication and cross validation. *Journal of the American Academy of Child Psychiatry, 21*, 564-569.

Rich, C.L., Young, D., & Fowler, R.C. (1986). San Diego Suicide Study: I. Young versus old subjects. *Archives of General Psychiatry, 43*, 577-582.

Robbins, D.R., & Alessi, N.E. (1985). Depressive symptoms and suicidal behaviors in adolescents. *American Journal of Psychiatry, 142*, 588-592.

Rotheram-Borus, M.J., & Trautman, P.D. (1988). Hopelessness, depression, and suicidal intent among adolescent suicide attempters. *American Journal of Child and Adolescent Psychiatry, 27*, 700-704.

Salk, L., Lipsett, L.P., Sturner,W.Q., Reilly, B.M., & Levat, R.H. (1985). Relationship of maternal and perinatal conditions to eventual adolescent suicide. *The Lancet, March 16*.

Shaffer, D. (1988). The epidemiology of teen suicide: An examination of risk factors. *Journal of Clinical Psychiatry, 49*, 36-41.

Shaffii, M., Carrigan, S., Whittingbill, J.R., & Derrick, A. (1985). Psychological autopsy of completed suicide in children and adolescents. *American Journal of Psychiatry, 142*, 1061-1064.

Spitzer, R.L., & Endicott, J. (1977). Schedule for Affective Disorders and Schizophrenia (SADS). New York State Psychiatric Institute, New York.

Welner, A., Welner, Z., & Fishman, R. (1979). Psychiatric adolescent inpatients: Eight to ten-year follow-up. *Archives of General Psychiatry, 36*, 698-700.

Wetzel, R.D. (1976). Hopelessness, depression, and suicide intent. *Archives of General Psychiatry, 33*, 1069-1073.

Chapter 5

Management

Simon Davidson, M.D., B.Ch.

Youth suicide has traditionally elicited reactions of horror and incredulity within the general population, associated with considerable concern. Qualitatively and quantitatively, the problem has reached serious proportions. Many questions remain unanswered; many theories are contradictory. The full spectrum of suicidal behaviors represents action, not an illness or disorder, and there is considerable heterogeneity amongst those who display it. There is not even agreement over whether there is homogeneity between suicide completers and attempters.

Yet despite the imperfections of the current body of knowledge, the problem has to be addressed and managed. With an issue such as this, causes and treatments are both unclear and probably multifactorial (Syer-Solursh, 1987). This chapter on management has been written from the vantage point of the "Crisis Intervention Model," which addresses management of the full spectrum of suicidal behaviors from the categories of Prevention, Intervention, and Postvention.

Prevention

The goal of prevention is to reduce the probability of suicidal behavior among currently unaffected individuals, and to promote early identification and treatment of those known to be at high risk. The increased incidence and prevalence of suicidal behavior makes it imperative that preventative measures be sought, as opposed to focusing solely on intervention.

In this section we will review, describe, and explore the utility of various preventative measures. One problem is that there is little empirical research to evaluate or compare their effectiveness; thus at present, ongoing funding of preventive measures is contingent upon subjective judgments of experts and the whims of policy makers. Scientifically sound evaluative and comparative research is very badly needed.

Professional Awareness

Professionals from several walks of life come into contact with children and adolescents, some of whom will fit into the spectrum that ranges from being vulnerable or at high risk for suicidal behavior, through actually carrying it out. Enhancing the expertise of these professionals in managing the problem predicts more efficient and effective prevention, intervention, and postvention.

The complex task of detection, assessment, and treatment of the suicidal patient requires a wide range of skills. Syer-Solursh (1987) has identified health care professionals (including physicians, nurses, psychologists, and social workers), and "gate keepers" (e.g., school personnel, clergy, police, and custodial personnel) as being the professional groups that could best benefit from enhanced suicide education and training.

The "gate keepers" are particularly important in prevention and in early identification of individuals requiring intervention and postvention. School personnel in particular have the greatest access over the longest time span to the youth population.

Increased professional awareness could substantially enhance all levels of suicide management. It is critical that there be inter-professional and inter-institutional collaboration between all groups. The utility of courses at the undergraduate level on suicide prevention is clear, as is the development of a minimal level of competence in related skills such as the assessment of risk. At the graduate level, the clinical skills required for dealing with suicidal individuals need to be taught. Substantiating these needs further, it should be noted that the majority of suicide victims consult their family doctors, usually about other concerns, in the months preceding the act.

Media Relations

Something that is true of any management initiative is that if a given intervention is found to *increase* the rate of attempted or completed suicide, it is having an effect contrary to its intent and should thus be discontinued or modified. This is particularly relevant with regard to the "imitation effect" by adolescents following exposure to media stories about suicide. The relationship between media people and health care professionals needs to be improved: the former should be educated about the dangerous potential of sensational journalism, and about how presentations on suicide, if paired with comprehensive information packages about available resources in the community, can curtail the imitation effect. Achieving a level of responsible reporting would allow the media to keep the public safely informed. Possibly such an approach could assume an important preventative role in enhancing public awareness, as discussed below.

Public Awareness

Public Education

Results from a questionnaire sent to professionals with experience in the field of suicide management indicated a strong recognition of the need for improved public education. Respondents recommended that programs be carried out in collaboration with media agencies, and that they incorporate such issues as reducing the stigma attached to seeking treatment for depression; informing the public about the warning signs of suicide; and familiarizing people with various coping skills to use in times of distress (Syer-Solursh, 1987).

School-Based Programs

Similar goals can be attempted through the development of school-based suicide prevention programs. However, the efficacy of such programs is controversial. Garland and Shaffer (1988) evaluated school based suicide prevention programs in the United States, and reported that:

- 95% were based on an incorrect theory: that is, that youth suicide is most commonly a response to extreme stress or pressure and could happen to anyone rather than usually being a consequence of mental illness;

- They were directed at 1600 students from schools in the eighth to twelfth grades, a large population in one sitting.

- They were of 1-2 hours duration, a brief period of time.

- They were taught by schoolteachers or community mental health professionals, a very limited intervention.

This study contended that although many teenagers would be *involved* in the programs, few suicidal individuals would thereby be saved, and several could actually be placed at greater risk. We can accept these conclusions, and contrast such programs with others that provide more positive results.

Given the above profile of a typical suicide prevention program, which includes in correct theory, large populations, brief interventions and solitary workers I would concur that such programs may indeed be dangerous. However, other types exist too, which incorporate interventional components with strong inter-professional, inter-institutional collaboration of health and education experts. The Ottawa Board of Education (1987), for instance, provides comprehensive, theoretically sound education about suicide to teachers, parents, schoolchildren, and a crisis intervention team that is trained to deal effectively with any school-based crises. All components of this program undergo evaluation, including the extent of past and present suicidal behavior of the target population before, immediately after, and six months after participation, compared with a control group not receiving the prevention program. For individuals of both groups identified as being currently at risk, the confidentiality code is broken and the students interviewed within 24 hours. Appropriate treatment within the school system or if necessary the local health system is obtained.

While the effectiveness of such a program still must be comprehensively evaluated over time, it is significantly different from those identified in Garland and Shaffer's "Profile." It is demonstrably safe; it identifies and treats individuals currently at risk, the majority of whom were previously unidentified; and it enhances knowledge and coping skills for most participants. Such preventative features do not necessarily apply only at the time of the program but, it is hoped, will consolidate over the years ahead and thereby have a preventative impact well into the future.

In summary, it is emphasized here that the school represents an environment that contains an important, accessible population amenable to comprehensive interventions. Of course, it must be recognized that school drop-outs, a possibly even higher risk group, are missed through such programs.

Suicide Prevention Centers and Hotlines

Although Bagley (1968) supported the efficiency of suicide prevention centers in a British study, other studies suggest there is no evidence that the introduction of such centers affects the suicide rate. They typically postvene or intervene, rarely prevene, and are not used by individuals most likely to kill themselves. What they *do* do is provide useful services in counseling individuals in psychological distress. They help to maintain individuals in their community and thereby prevent hospitalization, and provide triage for more extensive community services when necessary (Bridge et al., 1977; Lester, 1972; Shaffer et al., 1988; Syer-Solursh, 1987). However, they do not prevent suicide and do not, therefore, affect the suicide rate.

Treatment of Psychiatric Disorders

The majority of individuals who commit suicide have shown evidence of a psychiatric disorder at the time of their death. In general, the presence of a psychiatric disorder correlates as a significant risk factor associated with the full range of suicidal behavior. Early detection and effective treatment would thus be important first steps in the prevention of suicide. This intervention has not been tested in children or adolescents; in adults however, a significant fall in incidence in subsequent suicide attempts following psychiatric treatment as compared with untreated patients has been demonstrated (Shaffer, 1988). Further, since multiple suicide attempts may increase the probability of eventually carrying it out, adequate facilities for psychiatric treatment could save lives.

Restriction of Lethal Methods

As Eisenberg (1980) noted, many suicidal acts are impulsive and rely on an immediately available method. This is particularly true of adolescents. Thus, a reduction in the availability of the various means of self-destruction could represent a very important preventative initiative.

The literature abounds with debate about whether removal of preferred methods reduces the probability of suicidal behavior, or whether individuals would simply seek other means. The substantial reduction in the toxicity of domestic gas supplies in Britain accounted for the large decrease in overall completed suicide rates during this period; however, suicide by other means increased. Syer-Solursh (1987) recommends that measures be taken to reduce the lethality and availability of instruments of suicide, such as more stringent control of the distribution of medications and limitations wherever possible on the accessibility of attractive hazards. Physicians can urge greater care in the prescription of narcotic and psychotropic drugs and limits on quantities of analgesic drugs sold over the counter (Shaw et al., 1987).

Summary

Given the increase and extent of youth suicidal behavior, it seems reasonable to attempt to prevene in order to reduce the need to intervene. Where prevention is not possible, the earliest possible intervention strategies (such as comprehensive school-based programs) should be implemented. The low density of the suicide problem in the general population makes it difficult to measure the impact of various preventative efforts, but this should not be an argument for allowing the focus to remain on intervention. Enhanced empirical research to evaluate and compare effectiveness of preventive measures should be encouraged.

Intervention

Intervention refers to management of all aspects of an ongoing suicidal crisis. We will focus here on this process, addressing it sequentially and exploring options at decision-making junctions. These include identification and management of the patient in the community, in the emergency room, on inpatient units, and on an outpatient basis inclusive of outreach programs. Various therapeutic modalities and techniques in assessment and treatment will be addressed, including important aspects of the therapist-patient relationship and treatment of various psychiatric disorders. Finally, research and evaluation of intervention methods will be reviewed.

The issue of assessment has already been considered, both in Chapter 2 on clinical aspects and in Chapter 4 on risk factors. Assessment is the first aspect of prevention, since it is necessary to recognize the manifestations of risk factors for suicide. The more high-risk factors present, the more at risk an individual may be for suicidal behavior. Evaluation of these factors is an extremely important task, and helps to underscore the major decisions involved in deriving a proper management plan.

Professional Awareness

Over the past few years there has been a dramatic increase in publicity, most notably through the news media, of suicidal behavior and completed suicide. As well, professionals in different walks of life have been made aware through their continuing education of the existence and extent of the problem of youth suicide. Nonetheless, many continue to fail to identify vulnerable or high-risk individuals. Case Vignette #1 is an example:

Case Vignette #1

Kathy, a fifteen-year-old girl, was continuing to oppose the divorce of her parents which had occurred ten years ago. One year ago she severed her relationship with her schizophrenic father. She was in continuous conflict with her unemployed stepfather, "who is not my father." This in turn was creating tension between Kathy and her mother and between the mother and stepfather. Increasingly, her parents limited Kathy's access to her supportive peer group "because she prefers them." Kathy's school performance had declined considerably in the past three months, congruent with increased intrafamilial tension; recurrent headaches for which she received analgesic medication from her family doctor; increased concern about her "daydreaming and depression" by her peer group who failed to convince her to see the school guidance counselor; and completion of three school assignments in which she chose the topic of suicide.

In the preceding twenty-four hours, her boyfriend broke off with her. Feeling hopeless and unable to access her supportive peer group, Kathy impulsively attempted to slash her wrists. Recognizing that this would not kill her, she premedicated and attempted to strangle herself late at night behind her closed bedroom door. On losing consciousness, she fell to the floor. The noise wakened her mother, who loosened the noose and took her by ambulance to the Emergency Room.

Instead of merely correcting the grammar on her essays on suicide, Kathy's teacher could easily have talked to her and/or sent her to the guidance counselor for evaluation. Kathy indicated that she would have seen the guidance counselor on her teacher's suggestion, but could not take the initiative herself. It is also exceedingly common for family physicians, more than any other health professional or agency, to encounter suicidal patients before the actual act. Murphy (1975 a, b) demonstrated that 81% of all suicide victims had been in the care of a physician within the prior six months, and further, that 91% of overdose suicide victims had been under the recent care of a physician and in over half the cases the physician had supplied by prescription the complete means for suicide. Hawton et al. (1982) found that 50% of adolescent self-poisoners had seen their doctor within one month and 25% within one week of attempting suicide. Physicians treating young people do not routinely screen for indicators of self-destruction or potential suicide, and obtain mental health consultation only for overtly suicidal patients (Hodgman & Roberts, 1982). Seriously depressed children are unidentified in patient care (Fine et al., 1986; Goldberg et al., 1984).

Almost everyone who seriously intends suicide will give some verbal or behavioral clues about this imminent action (Ottawa Board of Education, 1987). Behavioral indicators are often manifestations of depression and may include several of the following symptoms:

- Loss of interest in former activities; withdrawal from social contact
- Difficulty in concentrating, problems with judgment and memory
- A dramatic shift in the quality of schoolwork and academic performance
- Feelings of sadness, emptiness and hopelessness, which may be expressed in the student's written assignments.
- Sleep disturbances, frequently insomnia but also hyper-somnia
- Overt expression of anger and rage, ranging from intense verbal outbursts to physical aggression

- Excessive use of drugs and/or alcohol
- Promiscuous behavior
- Uncharacteristic delinquent behavior; thrill-seeking
- Absence of known deterrents, such as friends and family.

Verbal or nonverbal communication indicators may include:

- Occurrence of previous suicidal gestures or attempts
- Statements revealing a desire to die or a preoccupation with death (may also be obvious in written assignments)
- Nihilistic comments; life is meaningless, filled with misery
- Verbal or written threats
- Gestures to be noticed (self-mutilation, scratches)
- Planning for death, making final arrangements, giving away favorite personal possessions
- Suddenly becoming cheerful after prolonged depression may represent "relief" that the decision is taken.

Management of the Suicidal Patient

We have identified the relative lack of professional awareness, and have focused on high-risk factors and warning signals as two important parameters in determining suicide risk and appropriate management. The following section incorporates these parameters with others. An attempt is made here to demonstrate in a practical way the decision-making process at the community level, at the assessment stage by the primary care physician in the office, in the Emergency Room, on the inpatient unit, and in outpatient follow-up.

Community Management

In the community, a child or adolescent experiencing overt or covert difficulty may come to the attention of friends, family, teachers, ministers, therapists and/or physicians. It is clearly demonstrated that teenagers in trouble most frequently turn to their friends. There are distinct differences in the level of expertise among the community members who can be turned to. However, certain basic principles remain the same (Ottawa Board of Education, 1987).

In the case of indirect disclosure by a youngster of suicidal intent — for example, revealed through a friend or a writing assignment — take the individual aside and strongly express your concerns, encouraging elaboration on any problems. In the case of a direct disclosure, maintain control. In both cases, encourage the expression of feelings, accept them, and avoid making judgmental comments or empty reassurances. The greatest single factor in preventing suicide is the knowledge that at least one person cares: empathize with the expressed feelings of distress, and give the clear message: "I want you to live."

All such situations must be taken seriously. It may be that others in the community with more expertise can better evaluate the seriousness and need for urgent help, and if in doubt, err on the side of caution. Do not leave the youngster alone. Avoid oaths of confidentiality! In life-threatening situations, what is revealed cannot be a secret: ensuring safety is far more important.

Emergency Room Management

Emergency Room visits by young people exhibiting suicidal behavior are quite frequent. McIntyre et al. (1977) found that such visits for children aged five to fourteen years occur five times more frequently than visits due to meningitis; Rauen-horst (1972) reported that 12% of emergency room visits are because of suicide attempts. Given this frequency, it is critical that emergency room "front-line" physicians become as familiar with the management of suicidal behavior as they are with other common emergency conditions.

The first line of management is to care for the medical consequences of the attempt. Then, at times in conjunction with medical care and at other times as soon as the patient's medical condition is adequately stable, the psychiatric component of care needs to be addressed. In some centers the emergency room physician is responsible for both medical and psychiatric decisions; in others, consultation to psychiatry, medicine, or pediatrics can be sought. Regardless of who does it, a comprehensive psychiatric assessment must occur before embarking on a course of management (see Chapters 2 & 4).

Based on the accumulated assessment information, plans for ongoing management can then be made. This will be on an inpatient basis if the individual is to be admitted for medical reasons. If medically possible, a decision must be taken regarding psychiatric admission and inpatient care, or discharge from the emergency room with or without follow-up. It is critically important to remember that even immediate follow-up — especially inpatient follow-up — should not curtail a comprehensive assessment and beginning treatment, right at the beginning in the emergency room.

Voineskos and Lowy (1985) have summarized the general principles of the management of a suicide attempt as follows:

- Preserve life — medical and surgical measures.

- Establish a therapeutic alliance with patient and relatives. Empathy, non-judgmental acceptance, and being prepared to listen are essential.

- Hospitalize when necessary — involuntary admission may be required. Treat psychiatric, social, and medical problems vigorously.

- When hospitalization is not necessary,
    - plan for crisis resolution,
    - provide or arrange for psychological and/or environmental support,
    - arrange for "lifeline,"
    - arrange for follow-up or referral.

Clinical Applications

Case Vignettes #2 and #3 provide clinical examples of two very different situations that require different approaches to management. Unfortunately most real situations encountered are not as clear-cut.

Case Vignette #2

Cindy, an intelligent, attractive thirteen-year-old, was brought to the Emergency Room by ambulance after a deliberate ingestion of 23 grams of acetaminophen. She had identified no serious problems until two weeks prior to the overdose. During this time, she had been arguing and fighting "about little things" with her family (consisting of mother, stepfather, three-year-old half-brother, and her maternal grandmother who had been temporarily living with the family for the past two weeks), and with her peers, including her best friend. The fighting was related to her mother's pregnancy and the birth of another half-brother two days prior to the overdose (the mother was still in hospital); to the associated intrafamilial tensions and pressures; and to a recent misunderstanding with her best friend. Feeling "mad at everyone," she impulsively decided to overdose, taking the analgesic medication but avoiding all the other medications available in the cabinet. She denied wanting to die and had considered no other method. Immediately after the ingestion, she called her best friend who made the necessary emergency arrangements.

There had been no deterioration in any aspects of her functioning and no other problematic or symptomatic behaviors. Cindy had no significant history of past medical, surgical, or psychiatric problems, and family history of psychiatric problems was essentially negative (except for a suicide attempt by the stepfather's sister many years prior). Aside from the problems identified previously, there was no evidence of severe underlying pathology in this well-reconstituted family. Cindy seemed comfortable in her relationship with her natural father, although he lived in another city and access was limited. Except for being angry at herself — "I was stupid and it won't happen again" — her mental status was aproblematic, depicting age-appropriate intelligence and insight. Diagnostically Cindy met the criteria for an Adjustment Disorder.

After the incident, reparation was made and friendship re-established with her friend. Through the family assessment, Cindy's relationship with her stepfather and mother was enhanced and acceptance of her new brother promoted. A beginning therapeutic alliance occurred between the psychiatric resident and Cindy and her family. In the absence of current suicidal ideation and intent, the low suicidal potential of the incident, and with family and peer support re-established and agreement made for immediate crisis intervention follow-up, Cindy was discharged in the care of her family after she had been medically cleared.

Case Vignette #3

David, a fifteen-year-old boy, was admitted directly to the Intensive Care Unit after ingesting about 3 grams of Carbamazepine, several Acetaminophen tablets and an unknown amount of alcohol. Since David was unconscious when admitted, the initial information was obtained from his family. He was living with his mother and older brother, his parents having divorced nine years previously. David had minimal contact with his father despite parental encouragement to the contrary, and blamed him for the divorce. There was a strong family history of psychiatric disorder, with brother and father being alcoholic and maternal grandmother having had a major depressive disorder.

In the six months prior to this crisis, David had become increasingly withdrawn from friends and family and had exhibited depressed affect. His family reported that during this time he had expressed feelings of worthlessness, his school performance had deteriorated significantly, he had complained of difficulty falling asleep, and he had lost some weight. He was increasingly upset about a seizure disorder for which he required Carbamazepine. He had never expressed any suicidal intent, and had no prior psychiatric contact. At home he was embarrassed by his alcoholic brother, and upset at his mother whom he perceived to be overcontrolling and intrusive. There was evidence of obvious problems with affective expression and communication within the family, even prior to David being ready to participate in the assessment.

On the evening of the crisis, the mother had questioned David about his very poor school performance. He had angrily withdrawn, apparently going to bed and closing the bedroom door. Several hours later, David's brother, who shared his room, retired. He noticed that David was having a "seizure," and that empty tablet bottles and a bottle of wine were lying on the floor next to his bed.

The family accompanied David to hospital in an ambulance. When medically able, David absolutely refused to provide any information. He turned his back, cried, and covered his head. He was presenting with a Major Depressive Disorder, several high risk factors, and high suicidal potential. Lack of rapport and inability to access current level of suicidal intent made it necessary initially to enforce the most stringent precautions outlined and David clearly required hospitalization. He gradually became more amenable to psychiatric assessment and treatment.

Inpatient Management

The decision to hospitalize a suicidal youngster is predicated upon several factors, which include:

- The presence of a continuing suicide risk in the immediate future, which can be well evaluated through utilization of the assessment previously elaborated. Weisman and Worden (1972) have developed the "risk-rescue" criteria to evaluate degree of lethality of a suicide attempt and the danger of a subsequent attempt. Information regarding the degree of risk includes: method used, degree of impairment of consciousness when rescued, extent of injury, time required in hospital to reverse the effects, and intensity of treatment required. Rescue circumstances include remoteness of help, type of rescuer, probability of discovery, accessibility to care, and delay between attempt and rescue.

- The presence of a major psychiatric disorder in conjunction with suicidal behavior. Examples include depression (Carlson & Cantwell, 1982), major affective disorder (Weiner & Pfeffer, 1983), and psychosis.

- The availability of psychosocial resources for the patient. These include available intrafamilial support systems (including evaluation of extent of intrafamilial psychopathology), community support systems (inclusive of available community-based outpatient resources), and the speed with which these can be accessed.

- The inability to obtain sufficient information from the patient and/or family in order to reasonably make a decision regarding hospitalization. It is strongly encouraged to err on the side of hospitalization if a decision cannot be taken for whatever reason.

Pfeffer and Plutchik (1982) evaluated the differences between child psychiatric inpatients and outpatients between the ages of six and twelve. Their findings were useful in elaborating parameters used in deciding upon hospitalization. The areas of difference between the groups were as follows: in comparison to the outpatients, inpatients exhibited more suicidal behavior, assaultive behavior, depression, anxiety, antisocial behavior, poor reality testing, frequent parental separation, severe parental assaultive behavior, parental depression and suicidal behavior, parental psychiatric hospitalization, and a more frequent history of prenatal and neonatal complications.

At times, the professional decision to admit a suicidal patient is opposed by the individual or his/her parents. In such situations admission may have to be arranged on an involuntary basis under prevailing mental health legislation, and since legislations differ it is imperative for professionals to be well informed of that applicable to their region. This will facilitate safe and legal inpatient management. Enforcing the legal process can be useful, since it both underscores the seriousness of the situation for patient and family and demonstrates that the hospital staff can protect them and will manage the serious situation at hand.

On-Ward Prevention Strategies for Ongoing Risk

There is obviously no guarantee that hospitalizing a suicidal patient will prevent the act. In the adult psychiatry literature, the rate of suicide in the discharged psychiatric population is higher than in the inpatient population, which in turn is higher than in the general population. Individuals on leave from hospital are also at higher risk. It is thus imperative that adequate suicide precautions be taken for psychiatric patients.

In considering the management of suicidal inpatients, certain precautions are strongly recommended. Inpatient units should develop suicide check lists, in order to protect patients from either intentionally or inadvertently harming themselves. The precautions listed should remain in effect until no longer necessary or until a revision is completed. The assessor completes, signs, and dates the form. Items included in such precautions are as follows:

- Level of nursing observation—one-to-one or close observation? If one-to-one, by whom should it be supplied: nurse, sitter, or a family member? Should it be maintained during visits by a family member or friend? If so, should that person be in the room or outside the door?
- Bathroom privileges—supervised or unsupervised
- Bathing privileges—supervised or unsupervised
- Clothing—hospital pyjamas or own clothing

- Sharp objects—remove, or may use if supervised

- Visitor restrictions

- Telephone calls—family, friends, or no restrictions

- Off-ward privileges—whether patient may leave the ward in the company of nurse, sitter, parents or family, hospital teacher, hospital staff or other.

- Smoking—whether or not patient may leave the ward to smoke, accompanied by whom, and how many times per day.

Regular re-evaluation of the patient's status forms an integral component of standard psychiatric care, and this is particularly necessary in order to update suicidal precautions. Ideally, the approach to precautions should encourage the development of one-to-one relationships through formal or informal individual and family therapy sessions. Both staff and other patients should be encouraged to reach out to the suicidal patient to exert the therapeutic power of interpersonal relationships, which have been shown to be unmatched by any other precautionary measure. The development of interpersonal relationships, communication, and a therapy aimed at dealing with conflicts, have demonstrated more positive outcomes (Syer-Solursh, 1987).

Farberow (1981) has suggested guidelines referred to as "suicide-proofing" a hospital. These include:

- Risk identification (e.g., watch for suspect behaviors such as hoarding medications)

- Safeguards (e.g., safety glass in windows, breakaway shower curtain rods, blocked access to roof)

- Communication relating to documentation and consultation

- Attitudes (e.g., avoid harsh, repressive measures)

These precautions are workable both on open and closed inpatient units and should be equally enforced in both situations. However, on an open unit the suicidal patient intent on running from the unit or who is being kept against his/ her wishes requires increased security and safety assurance.

Goals of Hospitalization

Contingent upon the needs of individual patients admitted for a variety of reasons, and upon pressure and demand for available resources, various philosophies have evolved in regard to the goals of hospitalization. As Syer-Solursh (1987) has indicated, extended hospitalization may not be necessary. Inpatient crisis intervention services typically keep suicidal patients for a period of three to five days to meet the following objectives:

- Completion of assessment in cases that could not be thoroughly assessed in the Emergency Department

- Stabilizing the patient's condition so that the therapeutic process can begin—that is, treatment of the underlying problems, for example psychiatric disorder or family dysfunction

- Temporarily removing the vulnerable individual from a highly stressful and deteriorating social situation

- Completing all necessary arrangements if longer inpatient stay or if long term treatment is necessary in special residential centers

- Involving all important members of the individual's support network, such as family, friends, and social agencies

- Making arrangements for the follow-up treatment plan

Pfeffer (1986) has provided a useful and self-explanatory list of tasks in the hospital treatment of suicidal children. Although she does not stipulate any time guidelines for these tests, they appear to address a hospitalization period in excess of the crisis intervention approach described above. The tasks are as follows:

- Protect the child from suicidal behavior

- Remove the child from environmental stressors

- Coordinate observations of a variety of therapists

- Offer multimodality diagnostic assessments

- Effect an immediate change in the family equilibrium

- Stimulate the child to maintain appropriate activities of daily living

- Support ego strengths and remediate ego deficits by a multimodality approach administered on a 24-hour basis

- Decrease the child's isolation by involvement with peers, school, and recreational activities

- Monitor treatment effects

- Plan discharge treatments.

Outpatient Management

Emergency room services for suicide attempters are generally good, particularly in terms of the employment of life-saving techniques. The extent of the medical emergency is not, however, a prognostic indicator regarding recurrent suicidal behavior. Individuals who have already demonstrated such behavior form a high-risk group whose completed suicide rates are higher than those of the general population, and outpatient follow-up is very important for this population. Greer and Bagley (1971) demonstrated that psychiatric intervention is associated with a significant reduction in subsequent suicidal behavior. However, substantial drop-out rates between discharge from the Emergency Room and outpatient follow-up are reported in the adult literature. Kreitman reported approximately 50% (Syer-Solursh, 1987) and Selkin found that only 16% and 21% of two separate samples actually showed up for their initial outpatient visits (Welu, 1977). Hence the development of "outreach programs" designed to initiate contact and treatment with the suicide attempter within a familiar environment, with a major emphasis on improving continuity and quantity of treatment received (Deykin, 1986; Welu, 1977).

Syer-Solursh (1987) has suggested that the following strategies could be employed to improve compliance of suicidal outpatients:

- Discussion and negotiation of referral should take place during the initial interview
- Specificity of appointment and source of referral
- A minimal waiting period before the initial appointment
- Ongoing systematic evaluation of the successful outcome of referral
- Consistent management of the patient could be exercised through effective communication between the agencies involved
- Recontacting patients after an initial interview could act as a reminder or provide for rescheduling

It would appear that it is only by a marked increase in follow-up care that a measurable impact can be made, both in terms of a reduction in the frequency of repeated suicidal behavior and in improvement of social well-being (Goldney & Burvill, 1980).

Approaches to Treatment

Once the necessary acute medical management and the safety of the patient have been assured, it becomes critical to have a planned mode of psychiatric intervention that promotes optimal, synchronous assessment and treatment to facilitate as good a prognosis as possible. Several aspects of assessment have already been outlined. All practical components of the psychiatric treatment may occur simultaneously and are embedded within theoretical foundations. To promote understanding, this section has been arbitrarily divided into the subsections of Integration of Therapeutic Modalities, Timing of Involvement, Therapist Qualities, Teaming, and Treatment of Underlying Psychiatric Disorder.

Integration of Therapeutic Modalities

The psychiatric treatment of suicidal behavior in children and adolescents is not well understood, and has been poorly studied both in terms of process and outcome research. There does seem to be some consensus among clinicians that a comprehensive evaluation is indicated in all cases of suicidal behavior, to allow for the planning of individualized management plans contingent on the data peculiar to a patient and his/her family. Further, there seems to be consensus about the use of a number of different therapeutic modalities. Family and individual therapy form the cornerstones of these modalities, with cognitive behavioral therapy, relaxation therapy, group therapy, and psychopharmacotherapy included in the management plan.

In individual therapy, some of the goals of treatment include: direct work in regard to suicidal behavior and underlying psychopathology, with derivation of an understanding of the forces and factors behind the suicide attempt (Teicher, 1979); developing appropriate coping strategies in management of stress and painful affect; attaining goals that would enhance self-esteem and diminish helplessness and hopelessness; and strengthening the child's positive relationship with the therapist and other supportive individuals (Pfeffer, 1984).

Family functioning and a family history of high risk factors can help to identify several characteristics that are significantly more common in the histories of children and adolescents experiencing suicidal behavior. Such factors include parental separation, divorce or death; single parents; family discord; parental unemployment; child abuse; and family history of psychiatric disorder inclusive of suicidal behavior. Inclusion of different permutations of these factors is the closest one can come to deriving common family characteristics. Idiosyncratic characteristics and problems pervading these families can only be identified and then treated through the process of comprehensive assessment. Sabbath (1969) does suggest that the degree of parental conscious or unconscious wish for the child's death, which the child interprets as their desire to be rid of him, may be an important contributing factor to suicidal behavior.

Timing of Treatment

In both individual and family sessions, timing of the initial phases of assessment and therapy are critical in terms of involving the relevant players in the process. A tendency of both suicidal individuals and their families is to deny the episode as quickly as possible, which permits everyone to reestablish their previous states, to maintain a homeostasis, and to resist change. If treatment is unsuccessful, the next efforts at resistance entail the family scapegoating the individual ("we're fine, it's all his/her problem"). This is done in an effort to protect the family system. The therapist's efforts to formulate the suicidal behavior in the context of a systematic hypothesis are resisted, and ultimately the family avoids treatment in order to avoid the threat of change.

Thus, the timing of psychiatric involvement is critical and intervention should occur as early as possible, in order to attain optimal management and the most favorable outcome. At the time of the suicidal crisis, the individual and family are most malleable: with later intervention there is an increasing risk of resistance, denial, and rigidity. Therefore, some involvement, even in the presence of a drowsy, nauseous, or even comatose patient, can provide an excellent catalyst to the assessment and treatment process. However, this approach is often inconvenient and unpredictable for the therapist. An early beginning to a therapeutic alliance and a rapid effort towards crisis resolution and change is aided with this approach. Continuity of care with the same psychiatrist or therapist is strongly encouraged. Where this is not possible, it is important that the family be made aware of the pending transfer as early as possible into the crisis assessment and treatment phase. Further, transfer must be expedited as smoothly and as quickly as possible, with the psychiatrist or therapist assuming the responsibility of the transfer. Such authors as Eisler and Hensen (1973) and Berlin (1970) support the crisis intervention approach, and Morrison (1969) and Turgay (1982) have applied it to dealing with suicidal youngsters and their families.

Once the therapeutic alliance and beginning work of the individual and family therapy have occurred in the manner outlined above, traditional scheduled ongoing therapy can occur on an inpatient or outpatient basis. As well, involvement of other therapeutic modalities can be integrated into the management plan.

Therapist Qualities

In providing emergency psychological support, Littman (1966) has recommended that the therapist must:

- Establish communication with the patient
- Remind the patient of his identity
- Involve the patient's family and friends
- Stimulate the patient toward constructive action.

He further suggested that psychological support is transmitted by a firm and hopeful attitude. Self-esteem or self-respect is the most basic psychic condition to be guarded if life is to continue. Shneidman (1976) among other authors, suggested the following practical features of the therapist-suicidal patient relationship:

- The therapist should stand as an ally for the life of the individual and, in a calm and gentle but firm and unequivocal way, make clear that his/her role is direct and active, including intervention to prevent suicidal behavior when the patient makes this known.
- This active relationship requires a delicate but deliberate violation of the usual confidence of the therapeutic relationship. Self-destructive plans are never to be held in confidence when their disclosure may prevent the death of the patient.
- Repeated monitoring of suicidal potential is an important feature of working with an actively suicidal patient.
- The therapist must have the capacity to allow the suicidal person to express the full range of the affect that is being experienced in all its pain and sadness.
- All efforts to reduce social isolation and withdrawal are essential. In this regard the active involvement of the family and surrounding network of the patient may be critical.
- Relationships, work, hobbies, and other individualistic activities enhance and maintain self-esteem.

- Coexisting psychiatric disorders must be evaluated and treated.

- If necessary, the therapist should seek consultation him/herself, as treating a patient with potential for completing suicide can be quite anxiety-provoking.

The need to balance consideration for patients' safety with the goal that they live their lives independently reminds us how limited the therapist's powers are. That is, they are no stronger than the patient's desire to make use of help. The therapist who appreciates his or her ultimate inability to stop the person who really wants to die is far more likely to be effective in restoring that person's sense of self-esteem and wholeness. Respect for independence, like the investment in the patient's well-being, is in itself therapeutic. Clarifying these limitations with patients helps convey respect for their autonomy, and reminds the therapist that a suicide can occur despite complete fulfillment of responsibility. Both parties are thereby better enabled to see that the risks of their mutual encounter are worth taking (Cassem, 1978).

Depending upon such factors as theoretical orientation and expertise of the therapist, and availability and level of functioning of a multi-disciplinary team, the patient and family can become involved with the same therapist or different members of the team in the modalities appropriate to their individualized management plan. This is equally applicable with inpatient and outpatient treatment.

Teaming

Successful, efficient, and effective management of the complex problem of suicidal behavior in children and adolescents requires comprehensive interventions of the types outlined above. In order to achieve this level of care with such a stressful group of patients, the availability of a well-functioning multidisciplinary team is essential. A broad range of expertise can be contributed by the team's constituent members. Voineskos (1975) acknowledges that an effective multidisciplinary team consists of medico-psycho-social input from staff of different disciplines, including at least a psychiatrist, a social worker, and a nurse. This team is the fundamental working unit of a psychiatric emergency service, particularly a crisis intervention oriented service. The members of this team can complement one another's talents and professional skills. Voineskos' (1975) description can be enlarged and generalized to fit both inpatient and outpatient programs.

This complex problem is not restricted to intervention only: it overlaps into prevention and postvention, which receive input from different professional groups and agencies while serving a similar population group. Efficient inter-agency and inter-professional collaboration enhances management of the suicide problem at all levels — prevention, intervention, and postvention. For example, good collaboration between the local school board and the hospital-based multidisciplinary team enhances efficiency and improves health care delivery in both prevention and intervention. The same would be true of the hospital-based multidisciplinary team and a self-help agency in the provision of intervention and postvention.

Treatment of Underlying Psychiatric Disorder

As mentioned, among the most significant high risk factors identified in suicide prevention are the presence of psychiatric disorder in the individual, and a family history of psychiatric disorder inclusive of suicidal behavior. Thus, optimal treatment of any underlying psychiatric disorder could prevent self-destructive behavior. The disorders occurring most frequently in children and adolescents include the full range of depressive disorders, conduct disorder, and drug- and alcohol-related disorders.

Although there is exciting research attempting to identify biological markers for suicidal behavior, it is premature to have established treatments. Montgomery et al. (1979) described a six-month double-blind flupenthixol decanoate/placebo control trial in patients with a history of two or more previous episodes of suicidal behavior, but excluding those with overt schizophrenia or depression. A highly significant difference was demonstrated at six months, with substantially less suicidal behavior in the flupenthixol group. However, while this study reports a prophylactic benefit from a drug it fails to take account of symptomatic or diagnostic differences in a hetero-geneous population. This study has not been replicated, and similar efforts with other psychopharmacological agents have not been pursued.

Research and Evaluation

Shaffer et al. (1988), Shaw et al. (1987), Syer-Solursh (1987), and Pfeffer (1986) confirm the abundance of sugges-tions in the literature regarding appropriate management of youth suicidal behavior, yet no methodologically sound study systematically evaluating such suggestions has been reported. Useful studies would compare outcome over a reasonable period of time with treated and nontreated groups, using standard measures before the start of treatment and at follow-up, and random assignment to treatment or placebo groups (Shaffer et al., 1988).

Summary

A number of psychotherapeutic modalities and treatment of the underlying psychiatric disorders by multidisciplinary teams can be used in various settings — outpatient, Emergency

Room, and inpatient. Practical considerations such as suicidal precaution checklists for inpatients, care through rapid follow-up, continuity of care, and outreach programs for outpatients are proposed. Finally, the need is stressed for studies that systematically evaluate different management approaches.

Postvention

Postvention focuses on management initiatives to be considered following a completed suicide. These initiatives are predominantly twofold, with a considerable overlap between them: the psychological autopsy, and postvention therapy. Both may involve any "significant others" including family survivors, close relatives, friends, school personnel, employer, family physician, or clergy.

Psychological Autopsy

Originally the psychological autopsy was used to clarify, for medico-legal certification, the manner of death (natural, accident, homicide, or suicide [Curphey, 1961]) through interviewing significant others in the victim's life. Wiseman and Kastenbaum enlarged its scope to review the terminal phase of the victim's life against the background of previous attitudes, life history, and modes of adaptation (Sanborn & Sanborn, 1976). With this broadened accumulation of data, research possibilities became apparent. It is hoped that information obtained from psychological autopsies will be useful in the planning of effective preventative programs and early interventional programs for others at high risk. Shaffer et al. (1988) proposed that the greatest preventative impact would come from effective intervention directed to teenage boys who have made a previous suicide attempt or who are depressed. Research findings by Niswander, Casey, and Humphrey (1973) demonstrated two recurrent themes. First, that as a consequence of the suicide, "a human wreckage of unresolved trauma" emerged. Second, that an invaluable therapeutic encounter occurred in the process of the psychological autopsy (Sanborn & Sanborn, 1976). Cain and Fast (1966) identified the isolationism experienced by the surviving spouse and the heightened incidence of psychopathology in the surviving children. It thus became evident that the survivors themselves formed a high risk group amenable to interventions, which therefore could be therapeutic and preventative simultaneously.

Postvention Therapy

As the psychological autopsy has evolved, its utility as a therapeutic tool among "significant others" has become increasingly evident. Postvention therapy consists of those activities that serve to reduce the after-effects of a traumatic event in the lives of the survivors. Its purpose is to help survivors to live more productively and with less stress than would otherwise be likely. The bereaved family represent a high risk group and form an important postvention population. Eisenberg (1980) suggested that the suicide of a child places a threefold burden on the survivors: grief at the loss, rage at desertion, and guilt at having failed.

A broad array of professionals are qualified to provide postvention management. Self-help groups with professional resources, such as bereaved family organizations, provide excellent ongoing support and therapy for survivors. Shneidman (1976) recommended the following tentative conclusions about postvention work:

- Therapy should begin as soon as possible after the tragedy

- The survivor-victims show little resistance and are most willing to work

- The role of negative emotions or emergency affect towards the deceased person needs to be explored, but not necessarily at the very beginning

- The therapist provides reality testing and acts as the quiet voice of reason. Given that this group is at high risk, their physical and mental well being must be carefully evaluated and re-evaluated. Postvention with this group can be viewed as prevention for the next decade or next generation.

Of the community-based "significant others" left behind, the school forms an important group. Adequate postvention at this level would include appropriate information sharing and discussion with relevant groups of students within the school, screening of individuals at high risk, and triage of carefully identified students into appropriate treatment. The type of work entailed here is done as a component of comprehensive school-based programs; that is, those programs that contain all aspects of comprehensive management of the suicide problem — prevention, intervention, and postvention. Shaffer et al. (1988) has correctly pointed out that there has been no systematic research in this area.

The professional health care group forms another important postvention group. In regard to psychotherapists whose patients have committed suicide, Littman (1965) reported reactions in the therapists as being similar to those found in others. In addition, however, therapists experience fears concerning blame, responsibility, and inadequacy. They can derive great psychological benefit from supportive consultation and case review with colleagues.

Summary

Schneidman (1976) identified that the consequences of suicide form a major public health problem and require the alleviation of the effects of stress in survivors whose lives are forever changed. The importance of postvention, which forms an integral component of the comprehensive approach to the management of suicide, cannot be overemphasized.

Recommended Reading

Davidson, Simon, I. (in press). Suicide. In Lorraine Sherr (Ed.), *Death, dying, bereavement and loss* (Chapter 6). London: Blackwell Scientific.

A helpful introduction to the topic, this is a comprehensive review of the problem of suicide in general with an emphasis on youth.

Goldney, R.D., & Burvill, P.W. (1980). Trends in suicidal behavior and its management. *Austr. and New Zealand J. of Psychiatry, 14,* 1-15.

This article evaluates all aspects of suicidal behavior though a critical review of the literature.

Klerman, G.L. (Ed.) (1986). *Suicide and depression among adolescents and young adults.* Washington, DC: American Psychiatric Press.

The Conference of Preventative Aspects of Suicide and Depression Among Adolescents and Young Adults of 1982 forms the basis of this book. Clinically relevant information about risk factors and strategies of intervention is included.

Roy, A. (1986). *Suicide*. Baltimore, MD: Wilkins and Wilkins.

An excellent, updated reference, which thoroughly and broadly addresses the problem of suicide across all age groups.

Shaffer, D., Garland, A., Gould, M., Fisher, P., & Trautman, P. (1988). Preventing teenage suicide: A critical review. *J. Am. Acad. Child Adolesc. Psychiatry, 27,* 6, 675-687.

This article extensively reviews the problem of teen suicide, including risk factors, prevention, intervention and postvention procedures. Research contributions are critically reviewed for all procedures.

References

Bagley, C. (1968). The evaluation of a suicide prevention scheme by an ecological method. *Social Science and Medicine 2,* 1-14.

Berlin, I.N. (1970). Crisis intervention and short term therapy: An approach in a child psychiatry clinic. *Journal of the American Academy of Child Psychiatry, 9,* 595-606.

Bridge, T.P., Potkin, S.G., Zung, W.W. et al. (1977). Suicide prevention centres. *Nerv. Ment. Dis., 164,* 18-24.

Cain, A., & Fast, I. (1966). The legacy of suicide. *Psychiatry, 29,* 406-411.

Carlson, G.A., & Cantwell, D.P. (1982). Suicidal behavior and depression in children and adolescents. *J. of Am. Acad. of Child Psychiatry, 21,* 361-368.

Cassem, N.H. (1978). Treating the person confronting death. In A.M. Nicholi (Ed.), *The Harvard guide to modern psychiatry*. Cambridge, MA: Belknap Press, Harvard U. Press.

Curphey, T. (1961). The role of the social scientist in the medicolegal certification of death from suicide. In N.

Farberow & E. Shneidman (Eds.), *The cry for help.* New York: McGraw-Hill.

Davidson, S. I. (in press). Suicide. In Lorraine Sherr (Ed.), *Death, dying, bereavement and loss.* London: Blackwell Scientific.

Deykin, E.Y. (1986). Adolescent suicidal and self-destructive behavior: An intervention study. In G.L. Klerman (Ed.), *Suicide and depression.* Washington, DC: American Psychiatric Press

Eddy, D.M., Wolpert, R.L., Rosenberg, M.L. (1987). Estimating the effectiveness of interventions to prevent youth suicides. *Medical Care, 25,* 12, 57-65.

Eisenberg, L. (1980). Adolescent suicide: On taking arms against a sea of troubles. *Pediatrics, 66,* 315-320.

Eisler, R., & Hensen, M. (1973). Behavioral techniques in family oriented crisis intervention. *Arch. Gen. Psychiatry, 28,* 111-116.

Farberow, N.L. (1981). Guidelines for suicide prevention in the hospital. *Hospital and Commun. Psych., 32 (2),* 99-104.

Fine, P., McIntyre, M.S., & Fain, P.R. (1986). Early indicators of self-destruction in childhood and adolescence: A survey of pediatricians and psychiatrists. *Pediatrics, 77,* 557-569.

Garfinkel, B.D., & Golombek, H. (1983). Suicidal behavior in adolescents. In H. Golombek & B.D. Garfinkel (Eds.), *The adolescent and mood disturbance.* New York: International Universities Press.

Garland, A., & Shaffer, D. (1988). *A national survey of adolescent suicide prevention programs.* Poster presented at the 35th Annual Meeting of the American Academy of Child and Adolescent Psychiatry, Seattle, Washington.

Goldberg, I.D., Roghmann, K.J., McInerny, T.K., et al. (1984). Mental health problems among children seen in pediatric practice: Prevalence and management. *Pediatrics, 73,* 278-293.

Goldney, R.D., & Burvill, P.W. (1980). Trends in suicidal behavior and its management. *Austr. and New Zealand J. of Psychiatry, 14,* 1-15.

Gould, M.S., & Shaffer, D. (1986). The impact of suicide on television movies: Evidence and imitation. *New England J. of Med.*, *315 (11)*, 690-694.

Green, A.H. (1978). Self destructive behavior in battered children. *Am. J. Psychiatry*, *135*, 579-582.

Greer, S., & Bagley, C. (1971). Effects of psychiatric intervention in attempted suicide: A controlled study. *Br. Med. J.*, *1*, 310-312.

Hawton, K., Cole, D., O'Grady, J., et al. (1982). Motivational aspects of deliberate self poisoning in adolescents. *Br. J. Psychiatry*, *141*, 286-291.

Hodgman, C.H., & Roberts, F.N. (1982). Adolescent suicides and the paediatrician. *J. Pediatr.*, *101*, 118-123.

Lester, D. (1972). The myth of suicide prevention. *Comprehensive Psychiatry*, *13* (6), 555-560.

Littman, R.E. (1965). When patients commit suicide. *Am. J. Psychotherapy*, *19*, 570.

Littman, R.E. (1966). Acutely suicidal patients: Management in general practice. *Calif. Med.*, 104-168.

McIntyre, M.S., Angle, C.R., & Schlicht, M. (1977). Suicide and self poisoning in pediatrics. *Adv. Pediat.*, *24*, 291-309.

Montgomery, S.A., Montgomery, D.B., Rani, S.J., Roy, D.H., Shaw, P.J., & McAuley, R. (1979). Maintenance therapy in repeated suicidal behavior: A placebo controlled trial. Proceedings of the 10th International Congress for Suicide Prevention and Crisis Intervention. Ottawa, 227-229. Reported in R.D. Goldney & P.W. Burvill (1980), Trends in suicidal behavior and its management. *Austr. and New Zealand J. of Psychiatry*, *14*, 1-15.

Morrison, G.C. (1969). Therapeutic intervention in a child psychiatry emergency service. *J. Am. Acad. Child Psychiatry*, *8*, 542-558.

Murphy, G.E. (1975a). The physician's responsibility for suicide: An error of commission. *Ann. Intern. Med.*, *82*, 301-304.

Murphy, G.E. (1975b). The physician's responsibility for suicide: Errors of omission. *Ann. Intern. Med.*, *82*, 305-309.

Niswander, G.D., Casey, T.M.and Humphrey, J.A. (1973). *A panorama of suicide*. Springfield, Ill.: Charles C. Thomas.

Ottawa Board of Education, Social Services Department (1987). *Suicide prevention program: A school-based prevention model*. Published for internal use.

Pfeffer, C.R. (1984). Modalities of treatment for suicidal children: An overview of the literature on current practice. *Am. J. of Psychotherapy, 38(3)*, 364-372.

Pfeffer, C.R. (1986). Psychiatric hospital treatment of suicidal children. In C.R. Pfeffer (Ed.), *The suicidal child*. New York: Guilford Press.

Pfeffer, C.R., & Plutchik, R. (1982). Psychopathology of latency-aged children: Relation to treatment planning. *J. of Nervous and Mental Dis., 17*, 193-197.

Phillips, D.P. (1974). The influence of suggestion on suicide: Substantive and theoretical implication of the Werther Effect. *Am. Social Rev., 39*, 340-354.

Phillips, D.P., & Carstenson, L.L. (1986). Clustering of teenage suicide after television news stories about suicide. *New England J. of Med., 315(11)*, 685-689.

Rauenhorst, J.M. (1972). Follow-up of young women who attempt suicide. *Dis. Nerv. Syst., 33*, 792-797.

Rosenthal, A.P., & Rosenthal, S., (1984). Suicidal behavior by preschool children. *Am. J. Psychiatry, 141*, 4.

Sabbath, J.C. (1969). The suicidal adolescent—the expendable child. *J. Am. Acad. of Child Psychiatry, 8*, 272-289.

Sanborn, D.E., & Sanborn, C.J. (1976). The psychological autopsy as a therapeutic tool. *Dis. Nerv. Syst., 37*, 1, 4-8.

Shaffer, D. (1974). Suicide in childhood and early adolescence. *J. of Child Psychology and Psychiatry, 15*, 275-291.

Shaffer, D., Garland, A., Gould, M., Fisher, P., & Trautman, P. (1988). Preventing teenage suicide: A critical review. *J. Am. Acad. Child Adolesc. Psychiatry, 27*, 6, 675-687.

Shaw, K.R., Sheehan, K.H., & Fernandez, R.C. (1987). Suicide in children and adolescents. *Adv. Pediatr., 34*, 313-334.

Shneidman, E.S. (1976). Suicide. In A.M. Freedman, H.I. Kaplan, & B.J. Sadock (Eds.), *Comprehensive textbook of psychiatry*. Baltimore, MD: Williams and Wilkins.

Syer-Solursh, D. (1987). Chairperson: Suicide in Canada. *Report of the National Task Force on Suicide in Canada*. Sponsored by the Mental Health Division, Health Services and Promotion Branch, Health and Welfare Canada.

Teicher, J.D. (1979). Suicide and suicide attempts. In J.D. Nospitz (Ed.), *Basic handbook of child psychiatry*, Vol. II (pp. 685-696). New York: Basic Books.

Turgay, A. (1982). Psychiatric emergencies in children. *Psychiatric J. of U. of Ottawa, 7*(4), 254-260.

Voineskos, G. (1975). Psychiatric emergencies: The crisis intervention approach. *The U. of Toronto Med. J., 51 (4)*, 85-89.

Voineskos, G., & Lowy, F.H. (1985). Suicide and attempted suicide. In S.E. Greben, V.M. Rakoff, & G. Voineskos (Eds.), *A method of psychiatry*. Philadelphia, PA: Lea and Febiger.

Weiner, A., & Pfeffer, C.R. (1983). *Cognition, depression and suicidal behavior in child psychiatric inpatients*. Paper presented at Annual Meeting of the American Orthopsychiatric Association, Boston.

Weisman, A.D., & Worden, J.W. (1972). Risk-rescue rating in suicide assessment. *Arch. Gen. Psychiatry, 26*, 553-560.

Welu, T.C. (1977). A follow-up program for suicide attempters: Evaluation of effectiveness. *Suicide and Life-Threatening Behavior, 7(1)*.

Index